Perspective Drawing

Perspective Drawing

Second Edition

Kenneth W. Auvil
San Jose State University

MAYFIELD PUBLISHING COMPANY
Mountain View, California
London • Toronto

Library of Congress Cataloging-in-Publication Data

Auvil, Kenneth W.

     Perspective drawing / Kenneth W. Auvil. — 2nd ed.
          p.   cm.
     Includes index.
     ISBN 1-55934-697-3
     1. Perspective.   2. Drawing—Technique.   I. Title
NC750.A98   1996
742—dc20   96-9382
                                            CIP

Manufactured in the United States of America
10   9   8   7   6   5   4   3

Mayfield Publishing Company
1280 Villa Street
Mountain View, CA 94041

Sponsoring editor, Janet M. Beatty; production editor, Julianna Scott Fein; manuscript editor, Janet Greenblatt; design and art manager, Susan Breitbard; cover designer, Andrew Ogus; manufacturing manager, Amy Folden. The text was set in 11/15 Janson and printed on acid-free 50# Finch Opaque by R. R. Donnelley & Sons Company.

Cover illustration and chapter opening art courtesy of Dover Publications.

Preface

This book grew from material I used in teaching a linear perspective segment in representational drawing classes. About thirty years ago it began as notes and slides for my own lectures, and, in time, I organized the data, diagrams, and procedures into a desktop-published reference book distributed by our university's book store. I have made extensive revisions of the book since then while using it in drawing classes.

The purpose of the book has not changed from that of the original desktop-published version—that is, to provide concise instruction on the basic principles of linear perspective. While the book is directed to the beginner who is just learning perspective drawing, it can also serve as a reference manual for those with advanced drawing skills. Too often I have seen advanced students make perspective errors that are inconsistent with high-quality drawing. Such slips are often grating incongruities in an otherwise excellent drawing. These students may have had an incomplete understanding of perspective principles from the start or may have forgotten some infrequently used but important perspective relationships.

Perspective Drawing can supplement studio instruction or serve as a guide for independent study of perspective theory. In either case, the theory must be accompanied by much drawing practice. A good procedure for students is to first read a chapter to get an overall view of the principles described and then make many drawings of simple objects. After the practice drawings, students can read the chapter again to make sure all the information is clear. Learning perspective theory is well worth the time because perspective is an essential factor in depicting objects in space with authority and conviction.

The sequence of topics in the chapters is much the same sequence I have used in my classes. The first six chapters are organized as pairs. Chapters 1 and 2 contain basic preparatory information; Chapters 3 and 4 introduce the perspective of rectilinear planes and solids: Chapter 3 deals with subjects that have horizontal and vertical edges, and Chapter 4 describes subjects with inclined edges. Chapters 5 and 6 describe circles in perspective: Chapter 5 introduces the circle plane, and Chapter 6 describes the cylinder.

The chapters do not have to be presented in this order, however. Chapter 4 may be studied after the circle and cylinder topics in Chapters 5 and 6. Chapter 7, *Using the Square as a Reference*, may also be used earlier in the sequence.

Chapter 8 is a supplementary chapter about cast shadows. An understanding of perspective is essential when plotting cast shadows, yet few books provide adequate information about it.

Appendix A describes a mechanical method for dealing with perspective. Appendix B, *Visualization*, is useful following Chapters 1 through 7 as a method of testing the understanding of perspective theory.

What's New?

Additional refinements are made in this second edition. Many new or revised illustrations will be found in all chapters; the text has been carefully scrutinized and modified throughout the book as well. Introductory statements in Chapters 1 and 2 have been expanded, new illustrations added, and several revised to improve the descriptions of some of the procedures or nomenclature used in perspective. Chapters 3 and 4 have had several major revisions in examples and associated text to clarify some of the perspective basics for horizontal, vertical, and inclined planes. Chapter 5 has improved a couple of the examples and parts of the text to clarify the circle in perspective. Chapter 6 has several new illustrations and some

text revision to clarify and demonstrate the perspective of the cylinder. Chapter 7 also has several revisions in examples and text to bolster the description of using the square and perspective square as a reference shape. Only minor revisions, primarily in the text, were made in Chapter 8, *Cast Shadows*, in Appendix A, *Mechanical Systems*, and in Appendix B, *Visualization*. Terms key to understanding perspective theory appear in bold type in the text and are defined in the new glossary at the back of the book.

Acknowledgments

I wish to thank those who reviewed the manuscript and provided useful suggestions: Stuart Baron, Boston University; Paul E. Berube, University of Massachusetts, Amherst; Hope Cook, Mankato State University; Chris Daubert, Sierra College; Jim Nawara, Wayne State University; Sarah A. Riley; Southeast Missouri State University; and John P. Stewart, University of Cincinnati.

Contents

Introduction

Perspective drawing is a method of working in two dimensions to create the illusion of a three-dimensional subject. The illusion may be presented as a drawing, painting, or other graphic work. Objects and their environments are depicted on a two-dimensional plane but appear as if viewed in real three-dimensional space.

What Is Perspective?

Perspective theory is often separated into two parts: linear perspective and atmospheric perspective. **Linear perspective** addresses how the shapes, edges, and sizes of objects change in appearance when seen at different positions relative to the observer. The distance between the object and observer, the attitude (rotation and elevation) of the object, and the viewing angle of the observer are all important in linear perspective.

The illusion of depth created by having objects overlap and by decreasing the size of distant objects is sometimes called **visual perspective.** Diminishing size and overlapping are closely related to concepts in linear perspective and are not treated separately in this book. In an elevated view of a city (Figure 1.1), diminishing sizes and linear relationships provide the visual cues for the illusion of depth and distance. Figure 1.2, meanwhile, is a dramatic example of the role of **convergence** in the illusion of depth, where the parallel edges of an object appear to merge in the distance.

Atmospheric perspective is used to identify other characteristics that convey how near or far an object is from the observer. A veil of atmospheric haze usually reduces the visibility of faraway objects (Figure 1.3). With distance, detail is obscured, contrast is reduced, and color is less intense. A variation in just one of these attributes changes the implied spatial position of an object relative to other objects (Figure 1.4). Atmospheric perspective is often used to add emphasis to linear perspective or depict depth even when the object is nearby.

The basics of perspective have been known since ancient times; overlapping, diminishing size, and atmospheric perspective can be found in art well over 1,000 years old. But it wasn't until the fourteenth century that perspective theory was analyzed in depth and its principles developed to a high degree of sophistication. Illusion reached a high point in the Dutch paintings and drawings of the fifteenth and sixteenth centuries. By that time, perspective theory had been mastered, and the first printed treatises on perspective are now about 400 years old.

The main principles of perspective are generally quite simple and relatively few in number. As a student of perspective, you have a big advantage over those studying more esoteric topics, because perspective occurs everywhere. It is

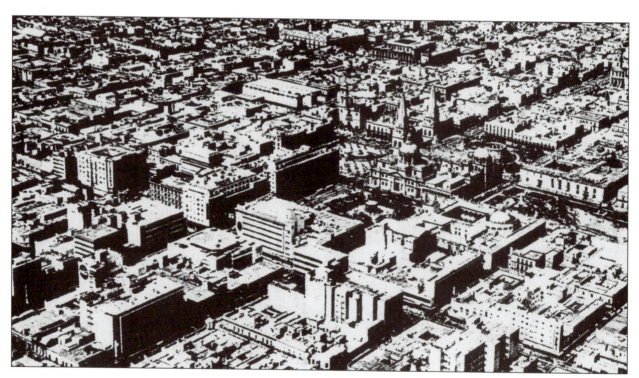

FIGURE 1.1
Linear relationships and diminishing sizes create the illusion of space and distance.

FIGURE 1.2
The apparent size of an object progressively decreases as its distance from the observer increases.

FIGURE 1.3
Atmospheric haze reduces value contrasts and detail in distant objects.

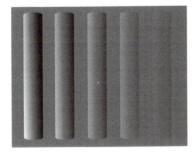

FIGURE 1.4
Diminishing value contrast affects our perception of space, even if other characteristics, such as size and detail are constant.

constantly visible and part of everyone's daily experience. For example, it strikes no one as odd that a person viewed from a distance of 100 feet appears as a very small image. If you measure with a ruler held up at arm's length, that person will probably measure less than an inch tall. You've probably also noticed that when you look down a long hallway, the other end appears very small (see Figure 1.2). Unconsciously, you know that the hallway is the same height and width throughout and that the change in apparent size is due to distance. Yet the diminishing of size with distance is one of the primary cues in the perception of real space relationships. Change in apparent size is the main basis for the theory of linear perspective.

Understanding perspective is critical for those whose graphic expression involves some degree of representation, from the near-abstract to the photographically realistic. For most artists, the final goal is **visualization,** the process of constructing an image of a subject that cannot be drawn by direct observation. The subject may not even exist. It may be imagined or derived from various forms of information, such as engineering plans or a verbal description. Visualization is involved when subjects can be seen but need to be redrawn from a different viewpoint, as when drawing a subject in a photograph or redrawing a subject to fit the perspective of a new environment.

While the principles of linear perspective entail a visual geometry that has mathematical precision, the experienced artist does not follow those precepts slavishly. In fact, artists often abstract or distort certain characteristics of their subject. Abstractions may be a simple matter of accenting or subduing certain parts of the drawing or eliminating or simplifying selected details. Distortion of perspective may be used to evoke certain sensory responses, infer a mood, suggest motion, or heighten the dramatic impact. Not only are artists selective about what they show of their subject and what they leave out, but they regularly distort, amplify, diminish, and disguise elements to achieve pictorial or expressive ends. The practice of bending the rules of perspective is widespread. A skilled artist, however, has a clear understanding of the basic relationships in perspective and knows to what extent they can be modified to enhance the image. To break the rules when you do not yet have a fundamental understanding of those relationships can result in images that appear naive and amateurish.

In creating an illusion, you must make certain compromises with how you actually view objects. You see subjects in the real world as an assemblage of parts, much like tiles in a mosaic. At any particular instant, you can focus on only a relatively small segment of the subject. To focus on other parts of the subject, you must shift your viewing direction, moving your eyes, head, or whole body. The subject may also be in motion. You seldom view a subject constrained by boundaries unless you view it through a window. You see it in full color and in three-dimensional space. Edges are visible because of perceptible breaks or sudden changes between values or hues.

When you draw the subject, you must select a fixed viewing direction, choose a limited portion of the subject to include in your drawing, and usually draw without color, often only in line. Artists and viewers accept these abstractions without much thought, for our long experience with paintings, drawings, photography, and other two-dimensional media have made us familiar with such forms.

This book is intended as a guide in using linear perspective in illusionistic drawing. However, no book can give you all the skills you need to make a convincing presentation; these skills come with experience, careful observation, and practice. The importance of practice cannot be overemphasized. The mechanics and theory presented here can help you understand perspective and provide a framework for creating perspective drawings and visualizations. The rest is up to you.

Perspective Terminology

Some of the terms used in describing how subjects are perceived and drawn have obvious meanings, while others are not so obvious. Here we define a few basic terms; others are defined in the book as they arise as well as in the Glossary.

Mass refers to the two-dimensional space, or area, that an object occupies in a drawing. The corresponding mass in the real object is its overall volume.

Proportion is simply a comparison of linear measurements in a subject. It often refers to the ratio between one major dimension of the subject and another, such as the total height of an object compared to its width (Figure 1.5). The proportion of a subject may be difficult to determine by eye alone, since the shape of the subject, its background, or other characteristics may confuse the eye. Even a practiced artist may need to check the proportion using a more objective technique.

The **station point,** or **viewpoint,** is the artist's location when viewing the subject. A drawing, to be consistent, is made as if the station point were a fixed location and the artist's

FIGURE 1.5
Proportion is the ratio between major dimensions in a subject.

eyes were kept in the same position—without moving from side to side or up or down—throughout the making of the drawing.

The **line of vision** is an imaginary straight line from the observer's eye at the selected station point to the subject (Figure 1.6). The line of vision usually ends at a central point in the area of the subject that is included in the drawing. The line of vision is an important reference in perspective relationships. Like the single station point, only one line of vision can be used for a consistent perspective in a drawing. You may have to shift your line of vision in viewing the subject, especially if the subject is too large to focus on all at once, but the drawing must still be made with that single line of vision as a reference line. The line of vision is described further in Chapter 2.

Right angle, horizontal, vertical, and *parallel* are all terms that have no special meaning in illusionistic drawing. In this book, however, the terms will usually refer to the way edges appear in the real subject rather than to how they appear in the drawing. For example, a right angle between edges in the subject would not be a right angle in a perspective drawing (see Figures 2.1 and 2.2).

A **right angle** is a 90-degree angle between two edges, such as an angle between adjacent sides in a square or rectangle. Boxes and architectural structures usually have many right angles. A right angle may also be used to describe the relationship between two planes or between edges and planes.

Horizontal describes a level (untilted) edge or flat plane, such as a floor, table top, or the top and bottom edges of a box on those surfaces. The surface of water in a basin or pond is a horizontal plane.

Vertical edges or planes are those at a right angle to a horizontal plane. The upright edges of doors or windows or the string of a suspended plumb bob are examples of vertical edges.

Parallel edges and planes are the same distance apart throughout their length. The classic example of parallel edges is railroad tracks. A **set of parallel edges** consists of all the edges in a subject that are parallel, whether the edges are in one object or many. If extended, these edges would never intersect or cross over one another. Chapter 3 describes how parallel edges of a subject are treated in a drawing to give the illusion of spatial depth.

Format refers to the border limits of the drawing. Usually the format shape is rectangular. A vertical format is longer top to bottom than side to side; a horizontal format is the reverse. Sometimes the vertical format is called a **portrait orientation** and the horizontal format is called a **landscape orientation.** A regular rectangle is considered the most appropriate shape for a format because it is the most neutral of all shapes. This undoubtedly evolved from our long experience with the "window" format of so many draw-

FIGURE 1.6
The line of vision is an imaginary line between the observer's eye and the subject.

ings, paintings, and photographs. We are less aware of the format when viewing subject matter within a rectangle than we would be if the "window" were a diamond, circle, oval, or even a square.

The Measuring Stick

Devices that aid in checking the relative size and position of the parts of a subject help tie together what the artist sees with the theory used to draw the illusion of that subject. The measuring stick is probably the most widely used device when drawing a subject. The stick has additional functions in aligning and extending edges and as a vertical and horizontal reference.

Artists are often depicted using a pencil or brush handle as a measuring stick. However, the variation in thickness and bulk of these instruments makes them awkward and imprecise tools for measuring or aligning. A more efficient tool is a slender dowel, wooden strip, tube, or wire that has a consistent thickness. A thickness of about ⅛ to ¼ inch is good, and a length of 12 to 15 inches is usually adequate. The stick should be perfectly straight and squared off at each end.

For measuring key dimensions in the subject, hold the stick at full arm's length (Figure 1.7). This is important because the distance between the eye and the stick must stay constant for all

measurements taken; any variation can result in error. Shut one eye when taking measurements, and always use the same eye for measuring parts of the same subject. Maintain the same distance between your eye and the subject until you complete all measurements. The distance from station point to subject must remain constant, even if you are drawing over several work sessions.

Hold the stick at right angles to your line of vision, whether measuring vertically or horizontally. As you look across the stick, line up its end with one edge of the object, such as the top edge, as shown in Figure 1.8. Adjust the tip of your thumb on the stick to line up with the opposite edge of the subject. Between your thumb and the top of the stick is one full dimension of the subject. Without moving the position of your thumb, rotate your hand and line up your first measurement on the stick with another major dimension of the subject, as in Figure 1.9. This gives you a comparison between one dimension of the subject and another dimension. In this example, the widest part of the subject is a little more than three-fourths of its height. Note that the first measurement was taken of the total visible height of the subject mass, from the back of the top rim to the near point on the base. Mass dimensions are the most important initially, since you need to know how much space the object will occupy in your drawing. Details of the subject

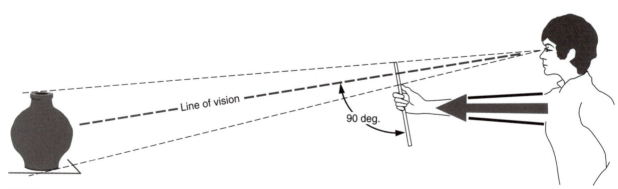

FIGURE 1.7
For measuring, the stick is held at full arm's length and at a right angle to the line of vision.

can be measured in the same way and compared with other measurements already established.

Your measuring stick can also help you determine the layout of your drawing. For example, use the stick to align selected edges or to check the position of one object relative to other objects.

Just align the stick with one of the edges of an object and then look for the places where the edge of the stick intersects other edges in your subject (Figure 1.10). Extending that same edge in your drawing in a straight line should lead to its intersecting other edges in a comparable way. Note

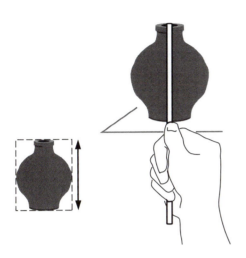

FIGURE 1.8
Using the stock for measuring, mark one dimension of the subject on the stick with your thumb.

FIGURE 1.9
Compare one dimension of the subject with the other dimensions to find proportional relationships.

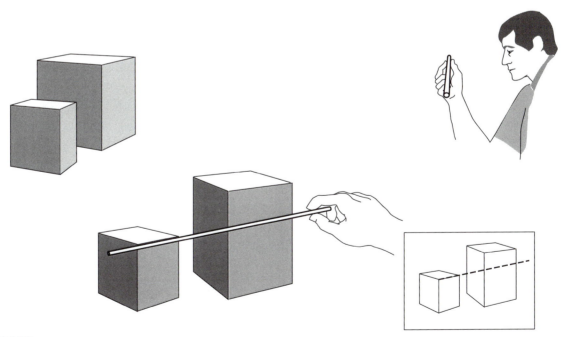

FIGURE 1.10
Aligning the stick with an edge in one object to find where an extension of the edge will intersect other objects. This technique can be used to check the relative position of elements in the drawing.

that it is not necessary to hold your arm stiff for this operation, nor is it important that the stick be exactly at right angles to your line of vision.

The stick can also be used as both a horizontal level and a vertical plumb, thus providing a reference to the horizontal and vertical edges of your drawing format. To use the stick as a level, hold the stick parallel to the floor, at right angles to your line of vision, and sight across its edge (Figure 1.11). Align the edge with some reference point in the subject. Note how other edges or points in the subject relate to the level edge of the stick. In your drawing, these same edges and points should have a comparable relationship to a line drawn parallel to the top and bottom of your format and passing through the same reference point.

As a level, the stick can help determine to what degree edges angle from a horizontal refer-ence. As in Figure 1.11, most horizontal edges in the subject will not be drawn as lines parallel to the top and bottom of your format. The same angle you see between the edge in the subject and the level stick should appear in your drawing be-tween the drawn line representing the edge and a reference line parallel to the top and bottom for-mat edges.

Finally, to use the stick as a plumb, hold it lightly at the top and let it hang vertically by its own weight (Figure 1.12). Because subjects often include a number of vertical edges, sighting along the vertical edge of the stick provides a check on the relative positions of remote verticals in the subject. The stick as a plumb can also check by how much an edge tilts off vertical in the subject. Compare what you see relative to the vertical edge of the stick to a vertical reference line in your drawing.

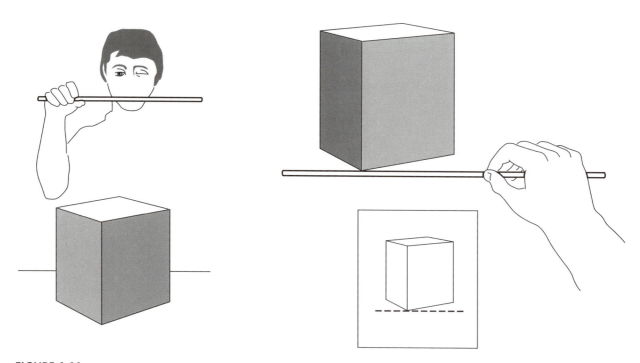

FIGURE 1.11
To use the stick as a level, hold it parallel to the floor and at right angles to your line of vision. Use it to compare edges in the subject to a horizontal reference.

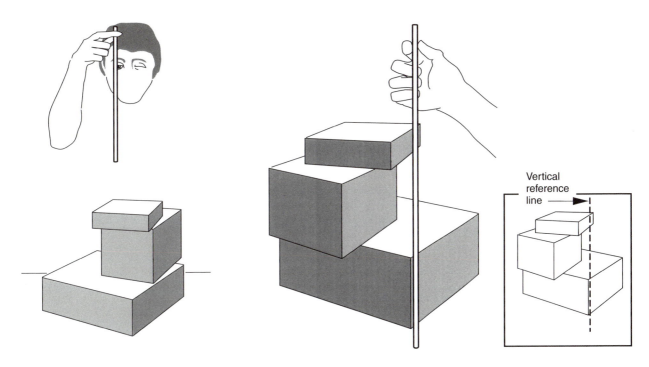

FIGURE 1.12
Using the stick as a plumb. The relative position of verticals can be compared in the subject and to a vertical reference in the drawing.

The Viewing Frame

Another useful drawing aid, particularly in the preliminary layout stage, is a **viewing frame** like the one shown in Figure 1.13. The frame can be cut from two small pieces of cardboard to the L shape shown in the figure. Each piece measures about 6 inches along the inner side of each leg. Equally spaced marks along the inner edge make the alignment between the two pieces easier and simplify finding key locations in the subject, such as its center point.

Adjust the two pieces of cardboard to leave a rectangular opening the same proportion as your drawing format. Clip or hold the legs securely together and sight through the opening to the subject. Keep the plane of the opening at right angles to your line of vision and the bottom and top edges parallel to the floor. The frame masks out

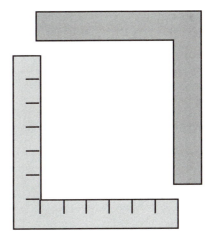

FIGURE 1.13
Components for a viewing frame. Cut from lightweight cardboard. Each leg is about 6 inches long. Optional marks on the inner part of the legs make alignment easier.

peripheral areas around the subject and allows you to test a variety of options in composing your subject within the format limits (Figure 1.14). Moving the frame closer to or farther from your eye exposes more or less of the subject within the opening in the mask.

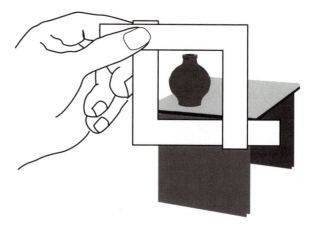

FIGURE 1.14
Using the viewing frame.

2

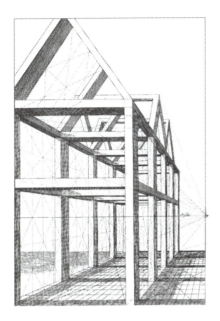

Some Perspective Basics

To learn how to translate objects viewed in real space to an illusion of those objects in a two-dimensional drawing, you need to become familiar with the terms that describe relationships in perspective. Some of the terms describe relationships in the subject being drawn; others describe relationships between the artist and the subject; and still others describe relationships in the drawing itself. In this book, the term *subject* will always refer to the real three-dimensional object chosen for the drawing.

Keep in mind that certain shapes in the subject must appear as different shapes in the drawing. For example, a circular form in a subject, such as a wheel or the top of a tin can, can rarely be drawn as a true circle. From all viewing locations except one, the circle in the subject is seen, and must be drawn, as an ellipse.

Parallel and Right-Angle Edges

Two terms frequently used in describing the principles of perspective are *parallel* and *right angle*. These terms usually describe relationships between edges in the subject. They can also refer to drawn lines representing the edges. The square in Figure 2.1 is drawn in its true physical config-

uration with opposite sides parallel and each corner a right angle (90 degrees). The square could be any of the three sides that are visible in the perspective drawing of the cube in Figure 2.2. In the perspective drawing of the cube, the lines representing the parallel top and bottom edges of the cube's square surfaces are not parallel, but are angled toward each other to give the illusion that the surface recedes, or moves back into space. The parallel opposite edges of the top surface also move toward each other, or *converge*. *Convergence* is the term used to describe the apparent diminishing distance between parallel edges of an object as they move farther away from the observer. Notice that the vertical edges in this cube remain parallel in the drawing; this is explained in Chapter 3.

Closely associated with convergence is **foreshortening.** This term refers to the apparent diminishing size of the width or height of an object as it angles away from the observer. For example, viewed from a fixed position, the proportion between the apparent height and apparent width of

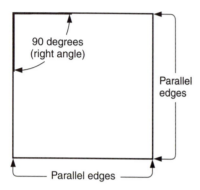

FIGURE 2.1
True parallel and right-angle edges.

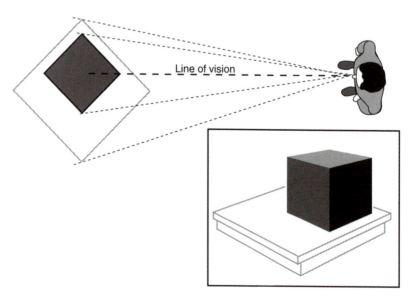

FIGURE 2.2
From most viewpoints, parallel edges and right-angle corners in a subject will not be drawn as true parallel and right-angle lines.

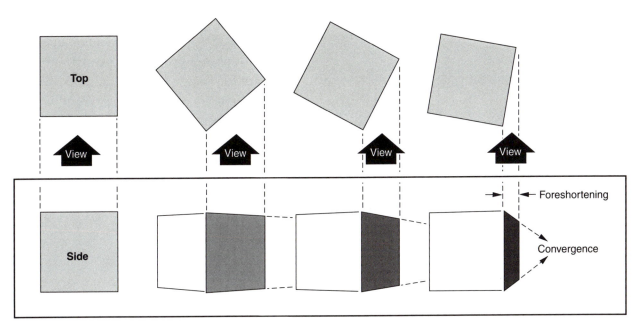

FIGURE 2.3
Convergence of parallel edges and foreshortened dimensions.

a square changes as the square is rotated in space (Figure 2.3). As you can see, the rate at which the edges converge has a direct relationship to the amount of foreshortening: The faster the edges converge, the greater the amount of fore-shortening.

Eye Level, Line of Vision, and Picture Plane

Eye level, *line of vision*, and *picture plane* are other terms that help describe perspective relation-ships.

Eye level is an imaginary horizontal plane exactly at the height of your eye. The eye-level plane is sometimes compared to the surface of the water in a large tank that is filled exactly to the level of your eyes. At that level, you see only the edge of the plane, as a straight horizontal line. All objects in your view are either below water level (below the eye-level line), above water level

(above the eye-level line), or partially submerged (intersected by the eye-level line).

Eye level rises and falls with the level of your eye, whether you are down near the floor (Figure 2.4), sitting, standing (Figure 2.5), in a tall build-ing, or in an airplane. The eye-level plane ex-tends an infinite distance in all directions and at a remote distance coincides with the **horizon**, which the eye level is often called. In your draw-

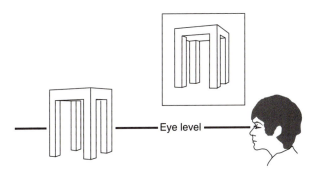

FIGURE 2.4
If the eye level intersects the subject, part of the object is above eye level and part below eye level.

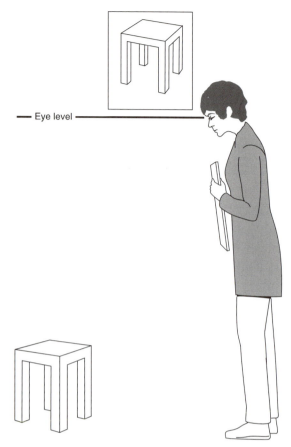

FIGURE 2.5
The subject may be entirely below or above eye level. The eye level changes with the level of the observer's eye.

ing, the eye level is a straight line parallel to the top and bottom of the format and in the same position relative to the drawing of the subject as your eye level is to the actual subject. The eye level in the drawing may be above, below, or intersecting the subject, as in the water tank example. The eye-level line may be on the drawing page or well off the page, either above or below the format borders.

The **line of vision** is a single imaginary straight line between your eye and the subject, as described in Chapter 1. It doesn't matter where on the subject the line of vision ends, but the center of the area being drawn is the logical place.

This location becomes more important when the subject encompasses a large amount of your field of view. To draw a subject with consistent perspective throughout, always remember to use a single line of vision.

Do not confuse eye level and the line of vision. The eye level is always horizontal and exactly at the height of the observer's eye. In a drawing, eye level is represented by a single straight line parallel to the top and bottom of the format. It will be located on the drawing page if the subject is at or near the same height as your eye. Eye level may be below or above your drawing page, depending on the relative location of the subject to your eye. This will be explained later in this chapter. The line of vision is an imaginary reference line between the eye and the subject. Think of the line of vision as a tube. If you look through the tube at your subject, the direction of the tube is the direction of the line of vision. It can angle up or down, depending on the direction you are looking. Only when you look straight ahead, neither up nor down, will the line of vision be aligned with your eye level.

The **picture plane** is an imaginary, transparent, flat plane between you and the subject. Think of it as a sheet of glass on which you could trace the outlines and details of your subject from a fixed viewpoint. The resulting drawing on the transparent sheet is what you will strive to replicate on paper.

The line of vision pierces the picture plane and is *always* at right angles to it. If the subject is situated at about the level of your eye, the line of vision may also fall on the eye-level plane (Figure 2.6). Such coincidences occur, for example, if you are drawing a standing human figure from a sitting position or if you are drawing other subjects that are approximately half above and half below your eye level. In this example, the eye level on the drawing is located near the center of the page and parallel with the top and bottom format edges.

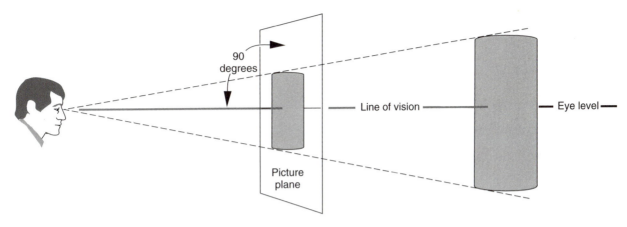

FIGURE 2.6
When you look straight ahead, the line of vision is at eye level. The picture plane is a vertical plane at a right angle (90 degrees) to the line of vision.

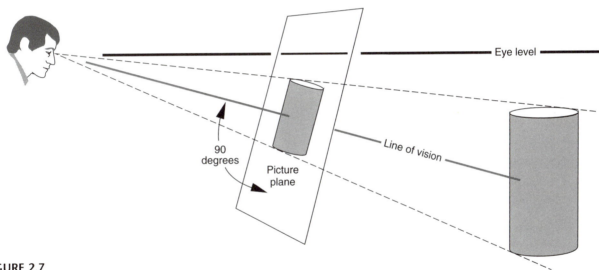

FIGURE 2.7
When you look down at a subject, the line of vision slants downward. The picture plane remains at a right angle to the line of vision. The eye level does not change.

Many of the subjects you draw will be below eye level. When a subject is below eye level, the line of vision is angled downward toward the subject (Figure 2.7). The picture plane moves with the line of vision and is still at right angles to it. However, the eye level does not change; it remains a horizontal plane at the height of the eye. The location of the eye-level line in this example is near the top of the drawing page and parallel

with the top and bottom format edges. The eye-level line may be located above the page if the subject of the drawing is a significant distance below the observer's eye.

An upward movement of the line of vision and picture plane occurs if the subject is above eye level. The picture plane and line of vision retain the same right-angle relationship to each other, and the eye level remains in place as a horizontal plane at the height of the eye (Figure 2.8). The eye-level line in this example is located near the bottom of the drawing page and parallel with the top and bottom format edges. The eye-level line may be located below the page if the subject of the drawing is a significant distance above the observer's eye.

The distance between the eye and the imaginary picture plane controls the scale of the image on the plane. Figures 2.6 to 2.8 show lines from the extremities of the subject to the eye. The points at which these lines pierce the picture plane show the extremities of the subject as projected on the plane. As the picture plane moves nearer to the subject, the size of the projected image becomes more nearly the size of the subject Figure 2.9. When the plane is *at* the subject, the image is the same size as the subject. The

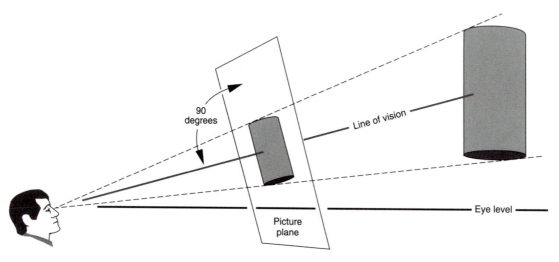

FIGURE 2.8
When you look up at a subject, the line of vision slants upward. The picture plane stays at a right angle to the line of vision. The eye level does not change.

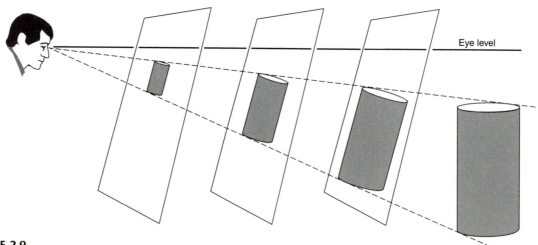

FIGURE 2.9
The size of the subject in the drawing is related to the distance between the eye and the picture plane.

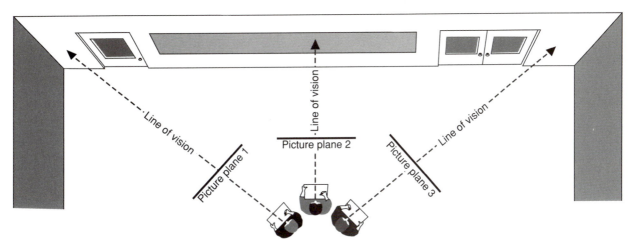

FIGURE 2.10
Overhead view of the room with three station points.

plane can also be located beyond the subject; in this case, the projected image will be larger than the subject.

Consistent Use of the Picture Plane

Earlier we said that to maintain consistency in perspective, you need to draw all parts of your subject using a single line of vision. Since the picture plane is fixed by the position of the line of vision, it follows that a drawing must use only one picture plane for all parts of the subject. What happens, then, if the subject is large and you need to turn your head, or at least shift your eyes, to see all parts of the subject clearly? Shifting the line of vision also changes the position of the picture plane. Since the amount of area you can focus on at any given moment is relatively small, a large subject may require several shifts of focus, each one shifting your line of vision and picture plane.

The overhead view in Figure 2.10 shows three viewpoints that an artist might take, represented by the three picture planes, in drawing portions of a large room. Each of the three views

represents an image of the room as the artist actually sees it. Each segment of the room is small enough so that it can be seen without significant changes in the line of vision or the picture plane. Looking toward one corner of the room, with picture plane 1, the artist would see and draw that corner of the room (Figure 2.11). Shifting the view to picture plane 2 would result in a different view and drawing (Figure 2.12) Finally, shifting to the other corner of the room, with picture plane 3, the artist would see and draw a third view (Figure 2.13).

FIGURE 2.11
Drawing of the room with picture plane 1.

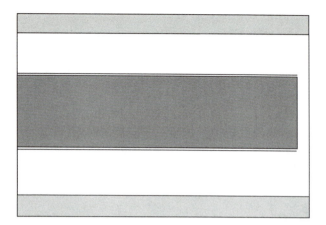

FIGURE 2.12
Drawing of the room with picture plane 2.

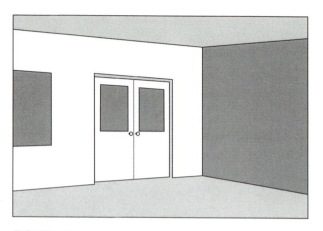

FIGURE 2.13
Drawing of the room with picture plane 3.

But what if the artist wanted to make a drawing of the whole wall? If the wall were drawn as the artist actually sees it, with a shifting line of vision to see the whole wall clearly, the drawing would look like a combination of the three individual drawings just described (Figure 2.14). Obviously, this would not be an accurate representation of the room, since the room does not have a bent wall. To draw the whole wall accurately, the artist would have to choose one of the three views, with one line of vision and one picture plane, and draw all of the subject with that reference (Figure 2.15).

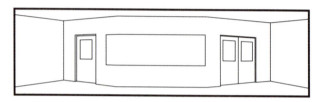

FIGURE 2.14
Composite drawing of the room with three lines of vision and three picture planes.

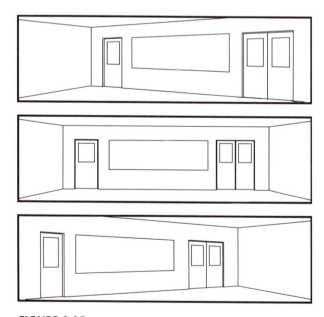

FIGURE 2.15
Drawings of three views of the room, each view using a single line of vision and one picture plane as a reference.

3

Edges in Horizontal and Vertical Planes

I f you extend any horizontal straight edge of a subject, such as the bottom edge of a box sitting on the floor, starting from the end of the edge nearest to you and projecting beyond the far end in a continuous straight line, the projected line eventually crosses eye level at a point called the **vanishing point** (Figure 3.1). All other edges of the box that are parallel to the first edge, if projected, meet at the same vanishing point. In other words, each set of parallel horizontal edges in the subject has a common vanishing point. In a simple rectangular form, such as a cube or box, there is usually a minimum of two vanishing points on eye level. (The only exception, described later, occurs with nonconverging edges.)

The cube in Figure 3.2 has two sets of parallel horizontal edges. Each set has three visible edges that project—or *converge*—toward a common vanishing point. Notice that the three visi-

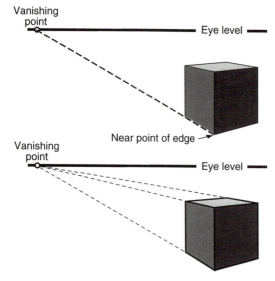

FIGURE 3.1
When you project one of the horizontal edges of the subject to the eye-level, all other parallel edges project toward the same point, or "vanish" in the far distance.

ble vertical edges have not been drawn as converging. Vertical edges often appear to converge so slightly as to be hardly detectable. It is often visually accurate to draw such edges as parallel in the drawing. (Sometimes, however, it is appropriate to converge parallel vertical edges, as we explain later in this chapter.)

A vanishing point may be shared with a number of edges from different objects in a drawing. Remember that all straight parallel edges in a subject have a common vanishing point, whether the edges are all on one object or on several objects. In Figure 3.3, for example, two objects are aligned so that the edges of one are parallel to the edges of the other, causing the edges in both objects to share the same vanishing points.

A drawing may have many vanishing points on eye level, one for each set of parallel horizontal edges in the drawing (Figure 3.4). One object

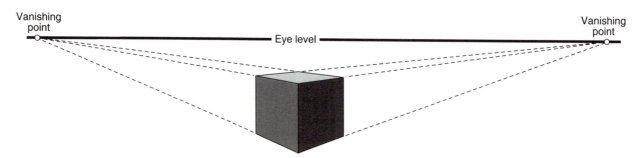

FIGURE 3.2
All horizontal edges of the subject that are parallel to each other project to the same vanishing point on eye level. A rectangular solid will have two or more sets of parallel horizontal edges. Each set has a separate vanishing point.

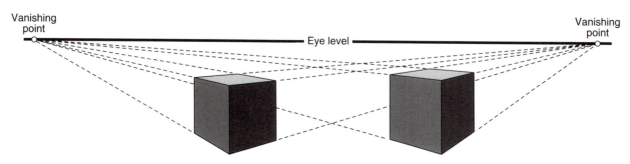

FIGURE 3.3
Each set of parallel edges has a common vanishing point, whether the edges are part of one object or many objects.

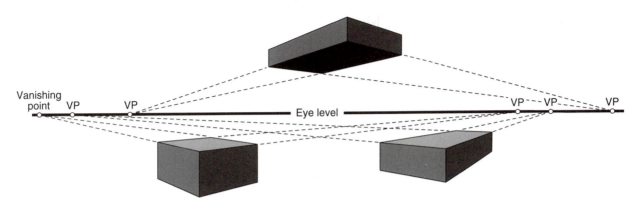

FIGURE 3.4
A drawing may have many vanishing points, one for each set of parallel edges in the subject.

may have several vanishing points if it contains several sets of parallel edges. A rectangular solid will usually have two sets of parallel horizontal edges.

Nonconverging Edges

If one set of parallel edges in the subject is parallel to the picture plane, the edges will not converge in the drawing. These edges in the subject do not recede from the picture plane in space, so they are simply drawn parallel to each other (Figure 3.5). The other two parallel edges of the subject, the sides showing at the top, are not parallel to the picture plane and have a vanishing point. Sometimes a single vanishing point is used in a drawing if many of the major edges of the subject are parallel to the picture plane. This arrangement is often seen in drawings of room interiors (Figure 3.6). The vanishing point is located near the center of the drawing for horizontal edges of the subject that are at a right angle to the picture plane. All other edges that are parallel to the picture plane are made parallel to each other in the drawing. This type of perspective layout is often called **one-point perspective.** (One-point perspective is compared with other perspective modes later in the chapter.)

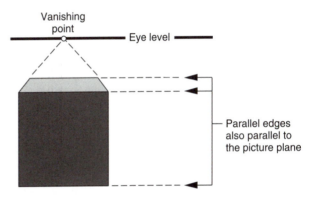

FIGURE 3.5
Parallel edges of the subject that are parallel to the picture plan do not converge and are drawn parallel.

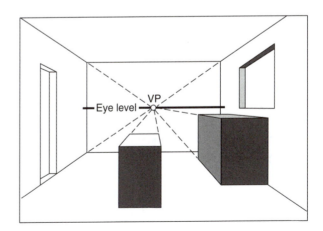

FIGURE 3.6
Some drawings are made with a centrally located vanishing point for one set of parallel edges. Other sets of parallel edges are drawn as if parallel to the picture plane.

Factors Influencing the Position of Vanishing Points

When parallel edges in the subject angle sharply away from the picture plane, their vanishing point may be located within the boundaries of the drawing, as in one-point perspective. Frequently, however, vanishing points are located some distance away from the drawing, to the left and/or right.

The location of the vanishing point to the left or right for any given set of parallel edges of the subject depends on two factors. The first and most important is the angle between the edges in the subject and the picture plane. The closer the edges are to being parallel to the picture plane, the farther away to the left or right the vanishing point for those edges will be. As noted before (see Figure 3.5), the edges of the subject that are parallel to the picture plane are not converged in the drawing because the vanishing point for the edges is, in effect, an infinite distance away.

In Figure 3.7, plane A angles sharply away from the picture plane. The top and bottom edges of the plane project to a vanishing point fairly close to the right of the subject. The top and bottom edges in plane B move away from the picture plane at a much smaller angle. They project to a vanishing point farther away to the right of the subject. Often, you will not be able to get all, or even one, of the vanishing points for a subject within the format of your drawing. With practice, however, you should be able to judge the rate of convergence accurately by the angle of the edges in the subject to the picture plane, even when the vanishing points fall well outside the borders of your drawing.

The other factor that influences the position of an object's vanishing points is the distance between the observer and the subject. The closer you are to the subject, the closer the vanishing points are to the center of the subject in the drawing and the closer together are the vanishing points for two or more sets of parallel edges. The farther you are from the subject, the farther away and the farther apart are its vanishing points in your drawing.

Drawing a subject from the same viewing direction but at different distances can alter the subject's appearance significantly in the drawing. In Figure 3.8, view A is drawn as if the observer were very close to the cube—in fact, unrealistically close. If vanishing points for edges that are at right angles in the subject are established too close to one another, the drawing will appear distorted. This is the same kind of distortion that occurs when a photograph of a subject is taken close-up but with a wide-angle lens. This kind of exaggeration is often seen in the drawings of beginning students who like to have both vanishing points on their drawing page. Experienced artists sometimes deliberately set vanishing points unusually close together to create a sense of dramatic scale in their drawing (Figure 3.9).

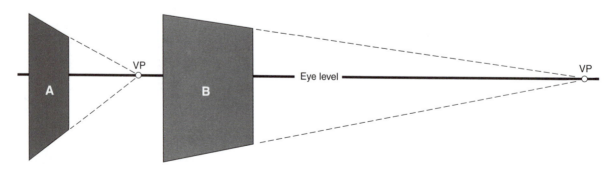

FIGURE 3.7
As the angle between planes in the subject and the picture plane increases, the vanishing point moves closer to a point directly behind the subject.

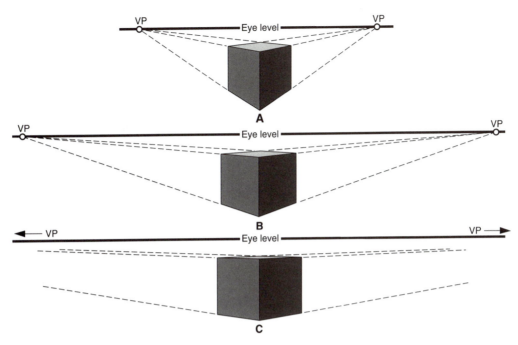

FIGURE 3.8
As the distance between the observer and the subject increases, the vanishing points move farther left or right and farther apart.

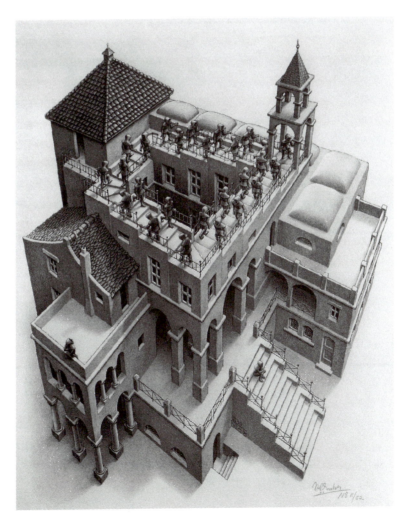

FIGURE 3.9
"Ascending and Descending,"
from *The World of M. C. Escher*
(Abrams, 1971)

Views B and C in Figure 3.8 have vanishing points that would result from more normal viewing distances. The viewer is closer to the subject in B than in C. A photographic parallel to view C would be a picture taken with a telephoto lens, where the subject appears flattened out, or reduced in depth—the opposite kind of distortion seen in view A.

Another way to view the effect that the distance between observer and subject has on the position of vanishing points is to examine what happens as the apparent size of the subject changes. When a subject is viewed close-up, its vanishing points appear close together relative to the size of the subject. As the subject moves farther away, its apparent size decreases and its vanishing points become farther apart relative to its size (Figure 3.10).

Converging Vertical Edges

As mentioned earlier, the vertical edges of subjects that are near eye level have insignificant convergence. These edges are usually drawn parallel to each other and to the left and right edges of the drawing format. However, vertical edges in a subject need to be drawn as converging if the subject is very far above or below eye level (Figure 3.11). How far above or below again depends on how close the viewer is to the subject. If the subject is farther away than it is above or below eye level, its verticals can be drawn parallel without appearing distorted. However, the test is in the appearance of the drawing. If distortion is evident, then you need to make an adjustment.

The vanishing point for vertical edges of a subject is directly above the subject if the subject

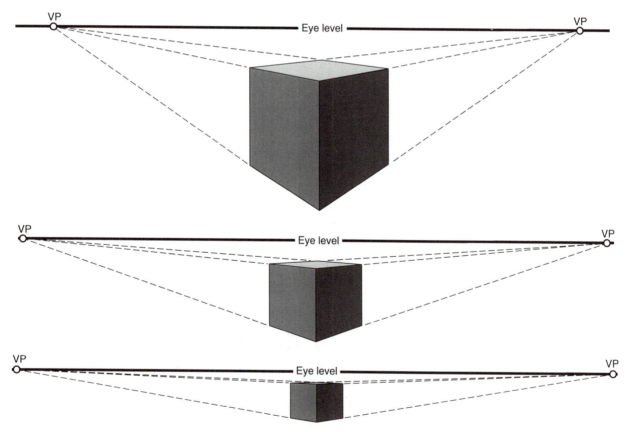

FIGURE 3.10
Vanishing points move farther apart relative to the apparent decrease in the size of the subject as it moves farther away.

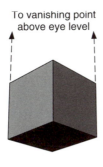

To vanishing point
above eye level

◄— Parallel —►

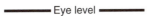

—— Eye level ——

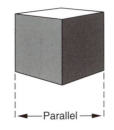

◄—Parallel—►

To vanishing point
below eye level

FIGURE 3.11
The convergence of parallel verticals in the subject is negligible when the subject is close to eye level. Draw vertical edges as converging if the subject is a significant distance above or below eye level.

is above eye level, or directly below the subject if it is below eye level. Verticals in several objects in the same drawing have a common vanishing point, usually directly above or below the center of the drawing format. Verticals of a tall object that extends through the eye level should have only one vanishing point or the object will appear bent in the drawing. It is usually better to draw such objects with the verticals parallel.

Failing to converge vertical edges on tall structures may result in the object appearing to expand in width as it gets farther above or below eye level, as in view A of the tall building shown in Figure 3.12. Note that in view B, the convergence starts below eye level even though the vanishing point for the verticals is above the structure. This is appropriate because the major portions of the vertical edges are above eye level.

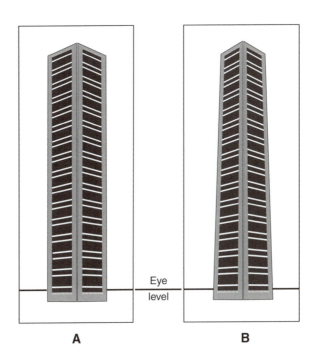

Eye level

A   **B**

FIGURE 3.12
Tall structures appear distorted unless verticals converge toward a vanishing point.

One-, Two-, and Three-Point Perspective Modes

In representational drawing, it is traditional to designate the perspective layouts as one-, two-, or three-point perspective. The three modes refer to the relationship of the picture plane to major components of the subject rather than to the number of vanishing points that may be used.

In *one-point perspective* (see Figure 3.6), a significant number of the edges in a subject, both horizontal and vertical, are treated as if they are parallel to the picture plane. Other major horizontal edges at a right angle to the picture plane vanish to a single vanishing point, usually near the center of the drawing. One-point perspective is often used by designers to depict room interiors or by artists who want to establish a view similar to looking at a stage from a center seat. This does not mean that all objects included in the drawing must use the same (or only one) vanishing point.

In *two-point perspective* (see Figure 3.8), the major sets of parallel horizontal edges in the subject are not parallel to the picture plane and have two or more vanishing points on eye level. The vertical edges are viewed as if parallel to the picture plane and thus are parallel in the drawing. As explained earlier, the parallel verticals in most subjects can be drawn without converging and not look distorted if the subject is not too far below or above your eye level. With most subjects you are likely to draw, you will probably be able to treat verticals as parallel to the picture plane.

In *three-point perspective* (see Figure 3.12B), parallel vertical edges in the subject are drawn converging to a vanishing point directly above or below the subject. Other parallel horizontal edges in the subject that are not truly parallel to the picture plane also converge to two or more vanishing points on eye level. Three-point perspective is needed if you are looking up or down at the subject or if the subject extends a significant distance above or below your eye level.

4

Inclined Planes

In Chapter 3, we said that parallel edges in horizontal planes, such as the top and bottom edges of a box, converge toward a common vanishing point at eye level. The only exception to this rule is horizontal edges that are parallel to the picture plane.

Parallel edges in a nonhorizontal plane, or **inclined plane,** such as the slanting edges of a tilted box or the inclined edges of a ramp, also converge toward a common vanishing point. However, the vanishing points for sets of parallel inclined edges are not on the eye-level line, since only horizontal edges have their vanishing point at eye level. Still, there is a direct relationship between the vanishing points for a set of parallel horizontal edges and the vanishing points for a set of parallel nonhorizontal edges if both sets of edges are in the same plane or in parallel planes .

It is important to observe carefully the actual relationship of edges in space. In Figure 4.1, lines labeled **a** represent parallel horizontal edges in the subject. These edges and other horizontal

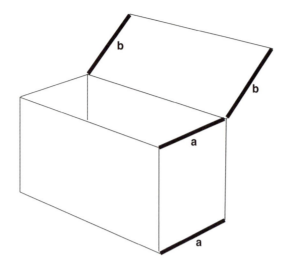

FIGURE 4.1
Horizontal edges **(a)** and inclined edges **(b)** in the subject.

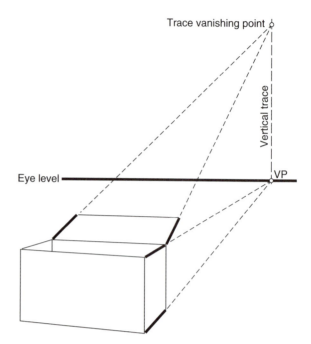

FIGURE 4.2
Parallel inclined edges converge toward a trace point above the vanishing point for horizontal edges.

edges parallel to them converge toward a common vanishing point on the eye-level line. Lines labeled **b** represent inclined edges in the subject. They converge toward a common vanishing point also, since they are a set of parallel edges, but their vanishing point cannot be at eye level, since they are not horizontal edges. These edges are slanting upward and converge as they move away from the observer. Their vanishing point is above eye level and to the right of the subject. The position of the vanishing point for the **b** edges bears a direct relationship to the vanishing point for the **a** edges. *The vanishing point for the b edges is aligned vertically above the vanishing point for the a edges* (Figure 4.2).

The Vertical Trace and the Trace Vanishing Point

The vertical line projected from the eye-level vanishing point is called a **vertical trace** or a **trace line.** The vanishing point for the parallel inclined edges in the subject (the **b** edges in our example) is called a **trace vanishing point,** or simply **trace point.** If the box lid is opened to a new position, changing the angle of the inclined edges, the location of the trace point on the ver-

tical trace will be higher or lower along the trace line (Figure 4.3).

So far, we have located trace points for one set of inclined edges on a vertical trace line projected from the vanishing point on the eye-level line. In more complex subjects, deciding which vanishing point to use to locate the trace point for a particular set of inclined edges can be more difficult. There might be several sets of parallel inclined edges or several vanishing points at eye level for horizontal edges—or both. Therefore, we must add the following parameter: *Parallel inclined edges in a subject converge toward a trace point directly above or below the vanishing point for horizontal edges that are located in the same or parallel planes.* In our box example, one of the **b** edges is in the same plane as the **a** horizontals (Figure 4.4). The other **b** edge is parallel to the first and is in a parallel plane, that is, in a plane with horizontal edges converging to the same vanishing point as the **a** horizontals. It is not necessary for sets of parallel inclined edges to be in the same plane as horizontal edges in a subject. If they are in planes parallel to the planes containing the

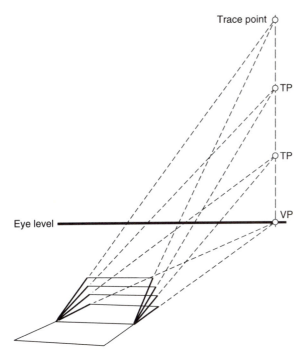

FIGURE 4.3
The distance between the trace point and the vanishing point increases as the edges are increasingly inclined from the horizontal.

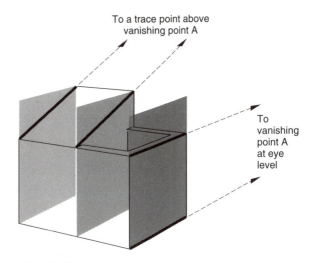

FIGURE 4.5
Inclined edges will converge toward a trace point above the vanishing point for horizontals in parallel planes.

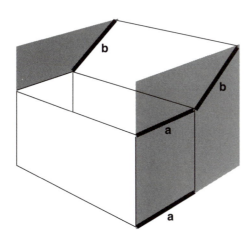

FIGURE 4.4
Horizontal and inclined edges that are in the same plane.

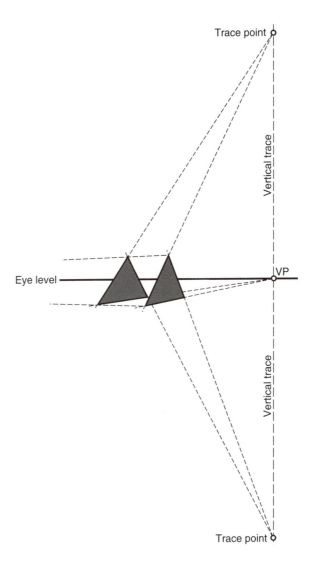

FIGURE 4.6
Trace points may be located above or below eye level.

horizontals, the rule for establishing trace points applies (Figure 4.5).

A trace line can project vertically above and below the eye-level vanishing point (Figure 4.6). The location of the trace point on the trace line depends on the angle and direction of the inclined edges in the subject. As the angle of the inclined edges in the subject approaches vertical, the distance of the trace point above or below the vanishing point increases. As the angle approaches horizontal, the distance decreases.

The distance between the subject and the observer affects the distance between the trace point and its parent eye-level vanishing point in much the same way as the observer's distance affects the vanishing points for horizontal edges of the subject (see Figure 3.8). For a given set of parallel inclined edges, the distance between the trace point and the eye-level line increases as the observer moves farther away from the subject.

Locating the Direction of Trace Points

When looking at a subject that has inclined edges, it is sometimes difficult to determine whether the trace point should be above or below its eye-level vanishing point or where the vanishing point is. This is often the case when the subject has no horizontals in the same plane or in planes parallel to the inclined edges. If the direction to the trace point is not obvious, start at the point on the edge that is closest to you and follow the edge; it will recede in the direction of its trace point. If parallel edges move upward and to the right, as in Figures 4.1 to 4.5, the trace point will be in that direction.

When an inclined edge is nearly parallel to the picture plane, it is often difficult to decide which end is closer. In these cases, it helps to imagine inclining the edge even further until it becomes apparent which end is moving farther away. In Figure 4.7, edge **ab** of the box on the left is slightly inclined from the picture plane. To verify that point **b** of the edge is closer, imagine the box tilted at an even sharper angle, as in the drawing on the right. The direction of the edge and its trace point becomes clear.

Note that in Figure 4.7, point **b** is closer to the observer than **a** only when the edge is tilted back far enough so that it is not parallel to the picture plane. When the edge is parallel to the picture plane (Figure 4.8, top), the two points are equally distant from the observer. When the box is rotated further down, then point **a** is closer to the observer. When a set of parallel inclined edges are almost parallel to the picture plane,

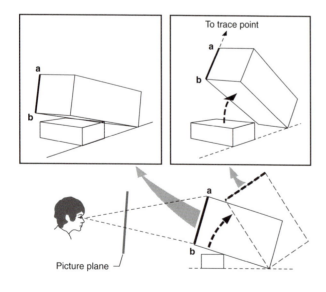

FIGURE 4.7
Finding the direction of the trace point for an inclined edge is simplified by rotating the edge to a greater angle from the picture plane.

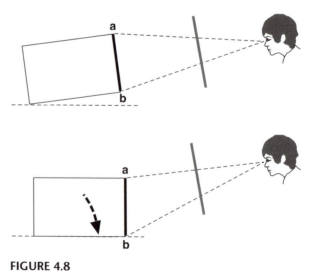

FIGURE 4.8
When the edge is parallel to the picture plane, points **a** and **b** are the same distance from the observer. When the edge is rotated downward, point **b** is farther away. The reverse is true when the edge is rotated upward, as in Figure 4.7.

they usually can be made parallel in your drawing without significant distortion.

The direction of the trace point for other inclined edges may be difficult to determine if the edges are nearly parallel to the picture plane. For edges that are nearly horizontal, an imagined horizontal rotation of the subject may be helpful. In Figure 4.9, edge **ab** in the left drawing is nearly parallel to the picture plane. From this view, end **c** of the box is barely visible unless the box is rotated so that **a** is farther away than **b**. Rotating the box further so that more of end **c** is visible will make the relative distance of points **a** and **b** more evident.

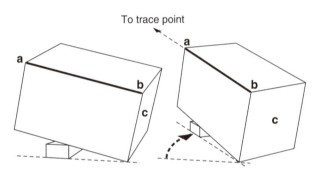

FIGURE 4.9
Finding the direction of trace points for inclined edges that are near horizontal is easier if the subject is turned so that more of end plane c is visible.

A trace point can be to the left or right of the drawing of the subject, depending on where its vanishing point is. The trace point may be above or below its vanishing point, depending on whether the inclined edge is receding up or down (Figure 4.10). The trace point may be directly behind the subject if the parent vanishing point on eye level falls there, as in a one-point perspective mode.

A Demonstration Set-Up

The simple set-up in Figure 4.11 is an easy way to demonstrate and practice locating trace points for inclined edges. Lay a yardstick or long straightedge along one side of a large box that is resting on the floor, as in the diagram on the left. The edge of the yardstick is in the same plane as side **p** of the box. Prop up one end of the box, as in the diagram on the right. Be careful not to shift the position of either the edge of the box still resting on the surface or the yardstick. Even though plane **p** has been rotated, the horizontal edge of the yardstick is still in the same plane.

Projecting the edge of the yardstick to your eye level will establish the position of its vanishing point. Since the horizontal edge of the yard-

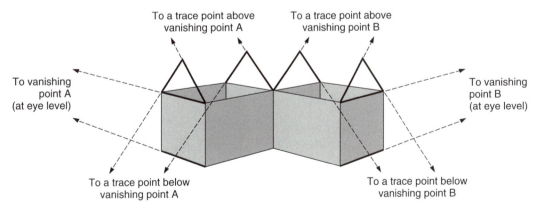

FIGURE 4.10
A subject can have multiple trace points above and below their parent vanishing points.

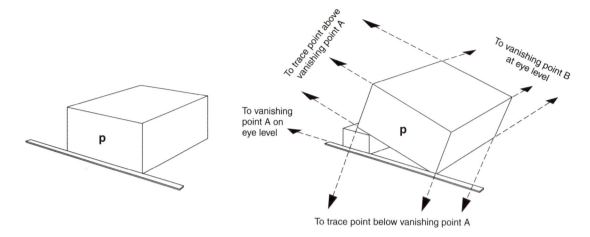

FIGURE 4.11
A method that can be used to establish a horizontal reference when no horizontals in the subject are in the same plane as the inclined edges.

stick is in the same plane as both sets of inclined edges of end **p** of the box, its vanishing point can be used to locate the trace points of those edges. The edges at the far end of the box that are parallel to the edges of end **p** will share the trace points with the corresponding edges of the near end. The third set of parallel edges is horizontal and converges toward a second vanishing point at eye level.

Applications

Knowing where a trace point should be for non-horizontal edges helps in drawing subjects that have a complex assortment of inclined edges, even if the trace point falls outside the drawing format. For example, in the stairway in Figure 4.12, the trace points for the angles of the stairway fall some distance above the vanishing points

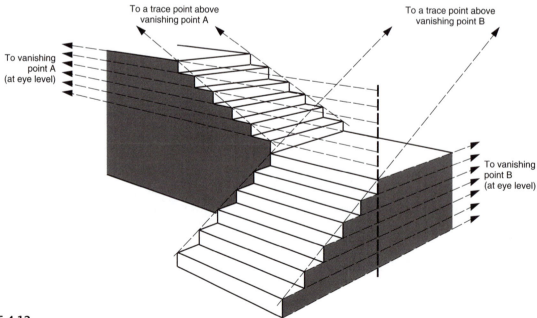

FIGURE 4.12
Using trace points to establish the convergence in stairs or ramps.

for the horizontals, themselves well to the left and right of the drawing of the stairs.

Note that the lines projected through the top corner of each step on the lower flight of stairs are continuous straight inclined lines that converge toward the same trace point. Since these lines fall in the same planes as the horizontal edges of the steps, the trace point is directly above the vanishing point for the horizontals. The same principle applies to the upper flight of stairs. Here the inclined lines have a different trace point, since they are moving in a different direction. Knowing the location of the trace points in relationship to the vanishing points for horizontal edges in a subject helps you to accurately gauge the rate of convergence for the inclined edges, even when their trace points are well beyond your format borders.

Inclined Ground Planes

The same principles apply in drawing inclined ground planes that move down and away from you, as in the downhill street scene in Figure 4.13. The layout for the subject is shown in Figure 4.14.

The parallel horizontal edges of the subject converge toward a vanishing point at eye level. The edges of the street, however, converge toward a trace point. Since the edges of the street in this example are in planes parallel to those containing the horizontals in the buildings, the trace point for the inclined edges falls directly below the vanishing point for those horizontals. If the slope of the street steepens or decreases, a new trace point will be needed for each incline change.

An uphill view (Figure 4.15) follows a similar structure, except the trace point is on a vertical trace above eye level (Figure 4.16). In this example, the inclined plane of the street moves upward through the eye level. The edges of the street converge toward a trace point above the vanishing point for the horizontals in the buildings.

The main principle to remember in dealing with inclined edges is that their trace points fall directly above or below the vanishing point for horizontals in the same plane or in parallel

FIGURE 4.13
Downhill street scene.

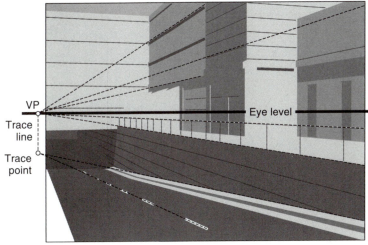

FIGURE 4.14
The edges of the street and some horizontal edges of the building are in parallel planes. The trace point for the street is below the vanishing point for horizontals in the buildings.

planes. If the subject has no horizontals in the same plane or in parallel planes to the inclined edges, you may need to establish a horizontal reference line, such as the yardstick shown in Figure 4.11. Project its edges to the eye-level line to establish the vanishing point. A drawing of a complex subject with different-angled planes may have several vertical traces, each with one or more trace points. As with many principles in perspective, when you understand the simple case, you can apply the same principles to draw more complex subjects.

FIGURE 4.15
Uphill street scene.

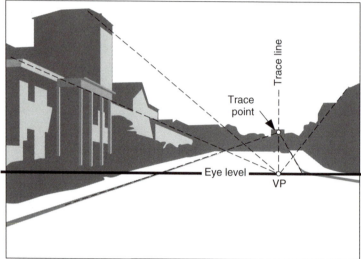

FIGURE 4.16
As in the downhill street scene, the edges of the street and horizontals in the buildings are in parallel planes. The trace point in this case is above the vanishing point for horizontals in the buildings.

5

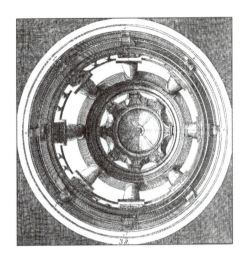

The Circle

Only when the plane of a circle in a subject is parallel to the picture plane can the circle be viewed as a true circle. The plane of a circle, like other planes, appears foreshortened if viewed at an angle to the picture plane, as in Figure 5.1. The foreshortened view of a circle is seen as a shape called an **ellipse.**

A straight line drawn across the widest dimension of an ellipse is called the **major axis.** A

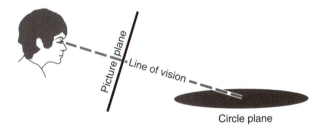

FIGURE 5.1
If the plane of a circle in a subject is at an angle to the picture plane, the circle is seen as an ellipse.

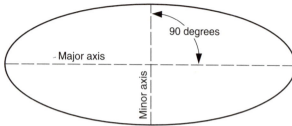

FIGURE 5.2
The major and minor axes of ellipses bisect each other at right angles.

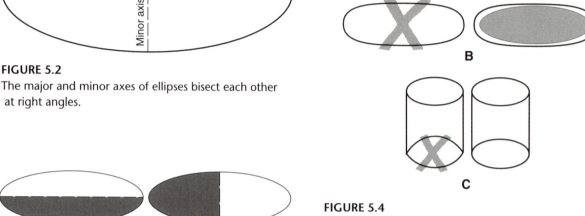

FIGURE 5.4
Some common errors in drawing ellipses.

FIGURE 5.3
Ellipses are symmetrical about their axes.

line drawn across the narrowest dimension of the ellipse is called the **minor axis.** The major and minor axes always bisect each other at their midpoints and are always at right angles (90 degrees) to each other (Figure 5.2). Both the major and minor axes are used to position ellipses accurately in your drawings.

Ellipses representing true circles in perspective are always symmetrical. If you fold an ellipse along either axis, the edges of one half fall precisely on the edges of the other half (Figure 5.3).

The ellipse is a smoothly changing parabolic curve. With a little practice, you should be able to draw very accurate ellipses freehand. Common errors in drawing the ellipse are shown in Figure 5.4. The football shape (A) is the result of narrowing the flatter part of the parabolic curve too rapidly, resulting in pointed ends. At the other extreme, narrowing the flatter part of the curve too slowly results in an ellipse that is too round at the ends (B). When drawing a cylinder, beginners often make an abrupt break in the curve at

the point where the side of the cylinder joins the end of the ellipse (C). If you have difficulty developing a feeling for the progressive changes in the elliptical curve, practice by tracing ellipses from photographs of circular objects. Once you become familiar with the character of the curve, you can easily detect inaccuracies in your drawing and make corrections.

Ellipse Proportion

The proportion of an ellipse is determined by the relative lengths of the major and minor axes. Circles in subjects are observed as ellipses of different proportions, depending on the position of each circle plane in relationship to the picture plane (Figure 5.5). Ellipses are described as fatter or thinner to indicate changes in proportion between the major and minor axes. They are described as bigger or smaller to indicate changes in the length of the major axis. Circle planes that are nearly parallel to the picture plane appear as

FIGURE 5.5
Proportion in an ellipse is the relationship between the length of the major axis and the length of the minor axis.

fat ellipses; the length of the minor axis is close to that of the major axis. As the angle between the circle plane and the picture plane increases, the ellipse becomes progressively thinner (the length of the minor axis decreases relative to the major axis).

From most viewpoints, circles in objects appear as ellipses. However, there are two exceptions. When the circle plane is parallel to the picture plane and the line of vision is near the center of the circle, the circle is seen and is drawn as a true circle (Figure 5.6). When the circle plane is at right angles to the picture plane *and* is in the same plane with the line of vision, the circle is seen as a straight edge (Figure 5.7). This is also true for circles in horizontal planes positioned at eye level (as in Figure 5.8).

Circles in Horizontal Planes

Circles that are in horizontal planes in the subject, such as the top and bottom of a cup sitting upright on a table, are the easiest to draw. Such circles are always drawn as ellipses whose major axes are parallel to the top and bottom of your drawing format. Once the major axes are established as horizontals in the drawing, the main problem is determining the relative proportions of the ellipses.

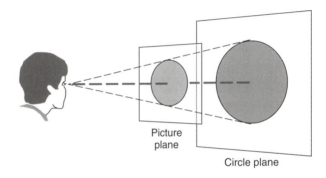

FIGURE 5.6
If a circle plane is parallel to the picture plane, the circle is seen as a true circle.

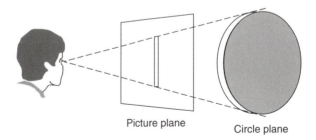

FIGURE 5.7
If a circle plane is at 90 degrees to the picture plane and aligned with the line of vision, the circle is seen as a straight edge.

If the circles are horizontal planes below eye level, the ellipses appear progressively fatter as the distance between the circle plane and eye level increases (Figure 5.8). The minor axes increase in length relative to the major axes. The same change occurs for circles in horizontal planes above eye level: The ellipses appear fatter as the distance between the circle plane and eye level increases.

At a given distance above or below eye level, an ellipse appears progressively thinner as the distance between the observer and the subject increases. The minor axis decreases in length relative to the major axis (Figure 5.9).

The Ellipse Axis and the Perspective Center

The center of a circle drawn in perspective coincides with the midpoint of an enclosing square drawn in perspective and is called the **perspective center** (Figure 5.10). The perspective midpoint of the square and the center of the circle are both located at the intersection of diagonal lines drawn between opposite corners of the square. The major axis of the ellipse representing

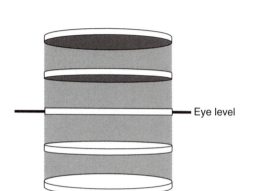

FIGURE 5.8
The minor axis will lengthen in relationship to the major axis as the distance between eye level and the horizontal circle plane increases.

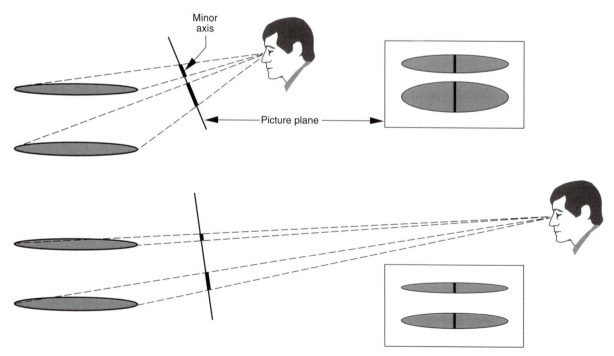

FIGURE 5.9
The length of the minor axis decreases relative to the major axis as the observer moves farther from the circle.

the circle always falls toward the observer, in front of the center of the circle. The edges of the ellipse touch the perspective midpoint of the square on each side, but these points are not at the ends of the major axis.

The distance between the major axis of the ellipse and the perspective center depends on the size of the circle and the distance between the circle and the observer. The observer sees the maximum width of the circle (the major axis) as the distance between the **tangent points** where projection lines from the eye meet the outer edge of the circle (Figure 5.11). As the observer moves away from the circle, the tangent points shift and the major axis moves closer to the true perspective center of the circle. If the observer is a long distance away and the circle is small in diameter, the major axis of the ellipse will be very close to the perspective center of the circle; however, the two never coincide exactly.

Increasing or decreasing the size of the circle affects the distance between the major axis and the perspective midpoint for the same reasons as changing the distances between the circle and the observer. The larger the circle or the closer the observer, the greater the distance between the major axis and the perspective center.

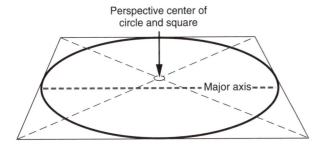

FIGURE 5.10
The major axis of the ellipse appears closer to the observer than the perspective center of the circle.

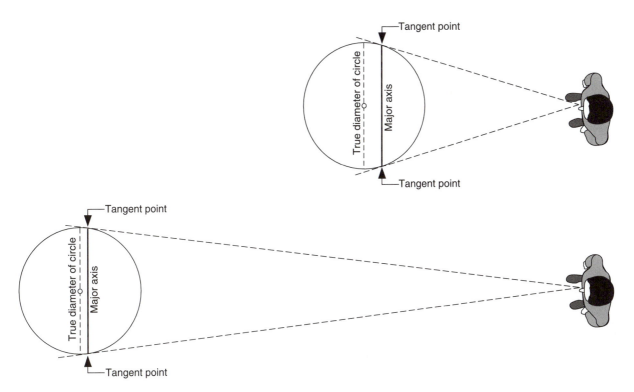

FIGURE 5.11
The distance between the major axis and the perspective center of the circle decreases as the observer moves away from the circle.

Rotating the Square with the Enclosed Circle

If the square containing the circle is rotated but still remains in a horizontal plane, the positions of the axes for the ellipse do not change (Figure 5.12). As described earlier, whenever the circle is in a horizontal plane, the major axis for the ellipse representing the circle is always parallel to the top and bottom of the drawing format.

Note in these examples that the major axis of the ellipse is always closer to the observer than the perspective midpoint of the square. The major axis of the ellipse is always parallel to the picture plane. The direction of the major axis has no fixed relationship to the direction of the diagonals or to the edges of the square. As the square is rotated to certain positions, the major axis may parallel one of the diagonals (C in Figure 5.12) or the front and back sides of the square (A). This occurs when those edges or diagonals are parallel to the picture plane.

Unlike the major axis, the minor axis always passes through the perspective midpoint of the square and the perspective center of the circle. As a result, the minor axis may coincide with one of the diagonals when the square is in a certain position (C).

Concentric Circles

Concentric circles are circles of different diameters that share a common center, as in the draw-

ing of the clock face in Figure 5.13. Many common objects, such as wheels or dials, have concentric circles that occupy the same plane. When this occurs, the circles drawn in perspective may look similar to the ones shown in the figure. Note

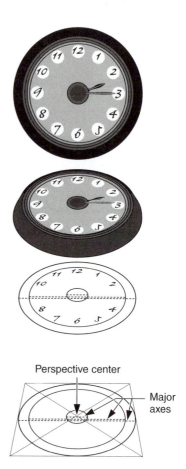

FIGURE 5.13
The major axes of ellipses for concentric circles are parallel. The axis for the small circle falls closer to the perspective center than the major axes for the larger circles.

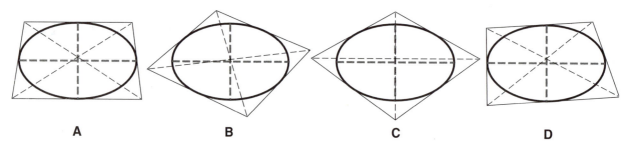

| A | B | C | D |

FIGURE 5.12
If the square enclosing the circle is rotated in the horizontal plane, the direction of the ellipse axes will not change.

that the three ellipses depicting the concentric circles do not share a common major axis, and none of the major axes pass through the perspective center of the circles. However, the minor axes do coincide and pass through the perspective center as well.

In ellipses depicting concentric circles, the major axis of a small ellipse is always closer to the perspective center than the major axis of a larger ellipse. The major axes of progressively larger ellipses are progressively farther away from the perspective midpoint. The major axis of an ellipse for a very small circle may *appear* to coincide with the perspective center—but it never really does. The distance between the major axes of ellipses depicting concentric circles decreases when the observer moves away from the subject. The distance between major axes increases as the observer moves closer.

The space between ellipses for concentric circles will be widest at the narrow ends (**a** in Fig-

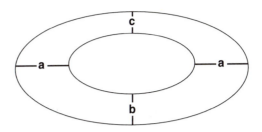

FIGURE 5.14
Spaces between ellipses for concentric circles vary. Space **a**, parallel to the picture plane, is wider than the foreshortened space **b**, even though **b** is closer to the observer.

ure 5.14). At this point, the major axes of the ellipses are parallel to the picture plane and spaces **a** are seen in their true width. The spaces between the ellipses along their minor axes are at an angle to the picture plane and are foreshortened. Space **b** is wider than **c** because it is closer to the observer.

6

Circles and Cylinders

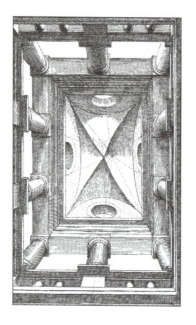

In Chapter 5, the major axes of most of the ellipses were drawn as horizontal lines. However, the major axis is a horizontal line only when the circle is in a horizontal plane. When the circle is tilted or vertical, the major axis of the ellipse will not be horizontal. There is one exception to this: when the ellipse axis of a tilted circle is horizontal; this exception will be explained later in the chapter.

Understanding the principles for drawing the cylinder will help you establish the correct direction for ellipse axes in your drawings. These principles can serve as a guide for drawing circles in any subject, even though the circles may not be the ends of cylinders.

To represent regular cylinders in any position relative to eye level and at any angle to the picture plane, you must first determine the direction of the cylinder's center line. The center line is an imaginary straight line between the centers of the circles at the ends of the cylinder (Figure 6.1).

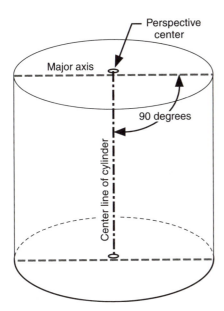

FIGURE 6.1
The major axis for an ellipse in a regular cylinder is at a right angle to the center line of the cylinder.

The center line is parallel to the sides of the cylinder and converges toward the same vanishing point. *The major axes of the ellipses for the ends of the cylinder will always be drawn at a true right angle (90 degrees) to the center line of the cylinder.* In Figure 6.1, the ends of the cylinder are in horizontal planes, and the major axes for the top and bottom ellipses are horizontal lines. The center line of the cylinder is vertical. Note that the bottom ellipse is drawn slightly fatter than the top ellipse because of its increased distance from eye level (refer to Figure 5.8). In most cases, the sides of the vertical cylinder can be drawn as parallel and vertical. If the cylinder is positioned very far above or below eye level, the sides of the cylinder should converge with the center line toward a common vanishing point. Follow the principle given in Chapter 3 (see Figure 3.10). If several cylinders with parallel center lines are involved, their sides will all converge toward a common vanishing point.

Circles in Nonhorizontal Planes

When the same cylinder is on its side or in other attitudes, *the major axis of each ellipse is always drawn at a true right angle (90°) to the cylinder's center line* (Figure 6.2). This is always true, no matter what the position, attitude, or elevation of the cylinder (Figure 6.3). Following this principle, most of the major axes of ellipses on nonvertical cylinders will be at an angle in your drawing.

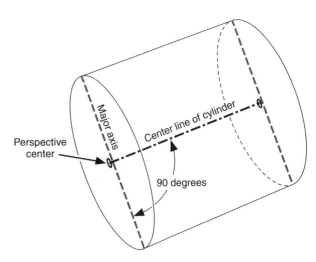

FIGURE 6.2
The major axis of the ellipse stays at a right angle to the center line when the cylinder is tilted.

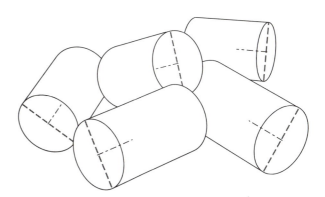

FIGURE 6.3
The relationship between the ellipse axis and the center line of the cylinder is constant, no matter what the attitude of the cylinder.

There are two exceptions: (1) When the center line of the cylinder is horizontal *and* parallel to the picture plane, the major axes of the ellipses representing the ends of the cylinder are true vertical lines parallel to the sides of the format in your drawing. (2) If the cylinder is tilted *and* its center line is in the same plane as the line of vision, the major axes of the ellipses are true horizontal lines parallel to the top and bottom of the format in your drawing.

Ellipses change in proportion, depending on the position of the circle in the subject relative to the observer's line of vision. If the circle is at a right angle to the picture plane and the line of vision is in the same plane as the circle, the circle is seen as a straight line (Figure 6.4). Circles in par-

allel planes positioned to the left or right of the line of vision become progressively fatter ellipses as their distance from the line of vision increases.

When circles are in parallel planes at an angle to the picture plane, as in Figure 6.2, the ellipse depicting the far circle is fatter than the ellipse depicting the near circle. *Ellipses for circles on the same center line are progressively smaller but fatter as they move farther away* (Figure 6.5). The sides of the cylinder converge with the center line toward a common vanishing point.

When circles are in the same plane at an angle to the picture plane, such as the front and rear wheels on one side of a vehicle, the circle that is farther away is drawn as a thinner and smaller ellipse than the near circle. *Ellipses for circles in the same plane are progressively thinner as they move farther away* (Figure 6.6).

The drawing in Figure 6.7 of four wheels of a cart depicts circles in parallel planes and circles in the same plane. A and B are ellipses depicting circles in the same plane. The wheel of the cart that is farthest to the right (B) appears as a thinner ellipse than the wheel closer to the observer (A). The minor axis of B is shorter in proportion to the major axis and the ellipse is smaller than A because it is farther from the observer. Meanwhile, C is in a plane parallel to and behind A, as is the far end of a regular cylinder. C appears as a

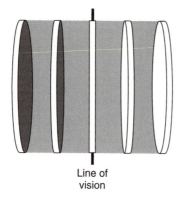

Line of vision

FIGURE 6.4
Ellipses for circles at a right angle to the picture plane will get fatter as they move farther to the left or right of a plane containing the line of vision.

FIGURE 6.5
Ellipses for circles on the same center line are progressively fatter as they move farther away.

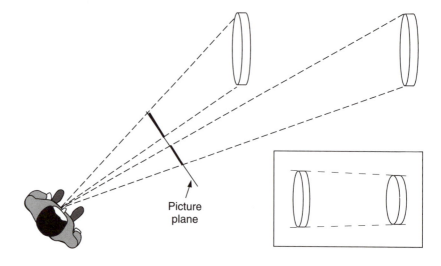

Picture plane

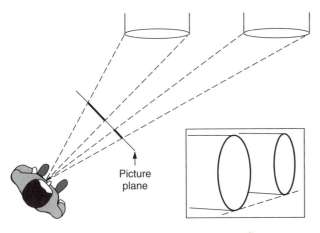

FIGURE 6.6
Ellipses for circles in the same plane are progressively thinner as they move farther away.

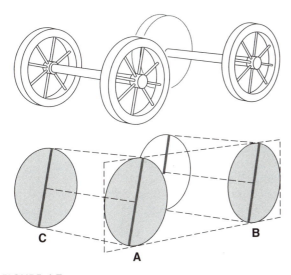

FIGURE 6.7
The proportions of ellipses change, depending on the location of the circles relative to the picture plane and line of vision.

fatter ellipse than A, and its minor axis of C is longer in proportion to its major axis. C is smaller than A because it is farther away.

Ellipse proportion changes progressively for circles in the same plane or in parallel planes as they move away from an observer on either side of the line of vision. In the row of cylinders in Figure 6.8, the ellipse for the near face A has a longer minor axis in proportion to its major axis than ellipse B. The ends of the cylinders between A and B have intermediate proportions.

Thus, the relative positions of the planes of the circles in a subject determine the relative proportions of their ellipses in the drawing. You can see this again in Figure 6.9, where the cubes are aligned so that A and B are in one continuous plane. B is a thinner ellipse than A, since it is farther away. C and D are in parallel planes, and the circles can be seen as opposite ends of the same cylinder. Ellipse D, being farther away, is smaller but fatter than ellipse C.

Whether the circles in a subject are in the same plane or in parallel planes, the amount of change in proportion between the major and minor axes of their ellipses is greater when the observer is close to the subject and becomes less as the observer moves away from the subject. When drawing, do not exaggerate such variations in proportion. Under most viewing conditions, the changes are subtle; large variations occur only if the observer is very close to the subject.

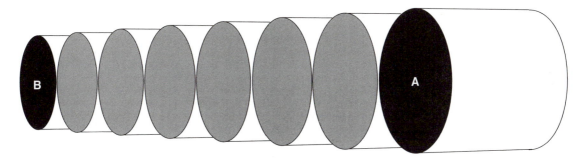

FIGURE 6.8
Circles A and B are in the same plane. Ellipse B is thinner than ellipse A, since it is farther away. Ellipses between A and B become gradually thinner and smaller as they move from A to B.

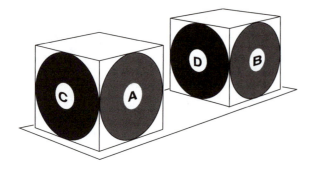

FIGURE 6.9
Ellipses A and B are in the same plane. B is a thinner ellipse than A because it is farther away. Ellipses C and D have a common center line. D is a fatter ellipse than C, since it is farther away.

FIGURE 6.10
Ellipses representing circles in nonparallel planes.

Figure 6.10 shows two sets of ellipses that are not in parallel planes. The wheels on the near side of the car are in the same plane. As in the cart in Figure 6.7, the ellipses representing the front wheel are slightly larger and fatter than the corresponding ellipses on the rear wheel. The ellipses representing the headlights share a separate plane at right angles to the plane of the wheels. The near headlight is slightly larger and fatter than the far headlight, as in the circles for the cylinders in Figure 6.8.

Other Cylindrical Forms

When drawing subjects that are not strictly geometric, you will be surprised at how often you can use the principles for drawing cylinders in perspective. The human body is a good example, with its tapered near-cylindrical arms and legs (Figure 6.11). Even the torso is basically a flat-

tened cylinder. Many other natural forms, such as trees (Figure 6.12), are also essentially cylindrical. Being able to depict the cylinder at different positions as it would appear in real space will be a great aid in translating the roundness and foreshortening found in a variety of natural forms.

FIGURE 6.11
Much of the human form can be seen as variants of cylindrical solids.

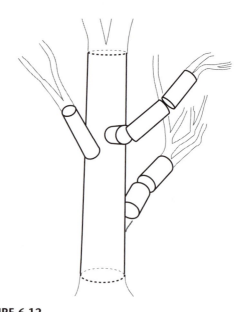

FIGURE 6.12
Visualizing the similarity between geometric and natural forms can aid in making a convincing spatial rendering of the subject.

7

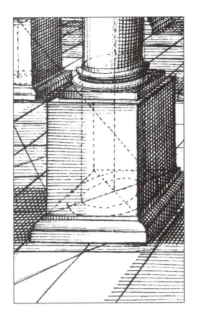

Using the Square as a Reference

When viewing a subject directly, you can visually estimate the proportion, foreshortened dimensions, or other measurements of the subject by using your measuring stick, as described in Chapter 1. But when drawing subjects that cannot be observed directly, such as those drawn from imagination or memory, you will need some other method to estimate how proportions in a subject change at various angles to the picture plane. The square is a reliable reference to use for this purpose.

Even when drawing objects that you are viewing, it is easier to judge foreshortened distances if the dimensions can be related to a square or increments of a square. Most objects, whether viewed directly or visualized from other sources of information, can be related to the square shape. In the house in Figure 7.1, the main mass of the front face is two large squares in proportion (A). The face of the right wing is a square

a

b

c

FIGURE 7.1
The proportions of most subjects can be determined by the square measurement.

from the foundation line to the eaves, and the left wing consists of two smaller squares from the foundation to the peak of the roof (B). What's more, other sections in the face of the building can be subdivided into squares or near squares within the whole (C). Having these squares as reference makes it much simpler to establish the correct foreshortening when drawing the subject at an angle to your picture plane.

The correct proportion of a foreshortened square can be judged quite accurately without a visible reference, no matter what its angle to the picture plane (Figure 7.2). Making these judg-

ments requires careful analysis of the rate of convergence of parallel edges in the square plane and the foreshortened dimension of that plane. Compare the foreshortening of the trio of planes in Figure 7.3. The same convergence rate is used for each square; only the foreshortened depth of the square is changed. In a second trio of squares in Figure 7.4, the foreshortening is constant but the rate of convergence changes. Notice how the plane appears to be a rectangle, either taller or wider than a square, when the relationship between the rate of convergence and the foreshortening of the plane is not correct.

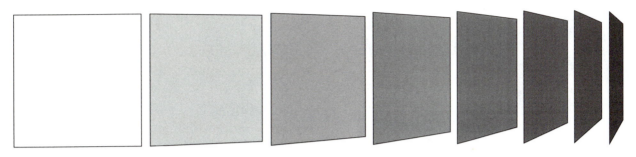

FIGURE 7.2
The correct proportion of a square at any angle to the picture plane can be judged quite accurately by visual assessment.

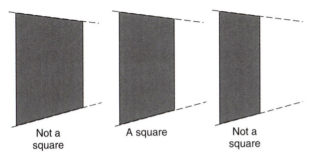

Not a square   A square   Not a square

FIGURE 7.3
Assessing the foreshortening of the square with a constant rate of convergence of the edges.

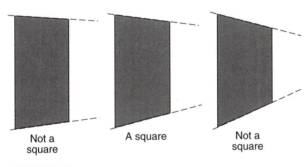

Not a square   A square   Not a square

FIGURE 7.4
Assessing the convergence of edges when the foreshortening is constant.

To use the square for a drawing reference, you must establish the correct relationship between its foreshortening and convergence. Ask yourself if your drawing of a square in perspective is a convincing illusion of a square or if it looks more like a rectangle. Most people can learn to recognize a true square in perspective.

Dividing and Multiplying the Square

Small variations from a square proportion can usually be estimated and drawn accurately. For example, if a subject is slightly taller than it is wide, use the square to establish the general proportion, then add a little to its height to match the amount the subject varies from the square.

If the subject varies significantly from a square proportion, you can divide the square into equal segments or use multiples of the square for additional reference increments (Figure 7.5). Using **diagonals** to find the perspective center of the square is the most accurate method of dividing the square into halves, as in A and B. Further divisions can be made using diagonals, as in C and D. Multiples of the square can be made using the method illustrated in E and F.

The intersection of the diagonals of the square is its true perspective midpoint, no matter what angle the square may be to your picture

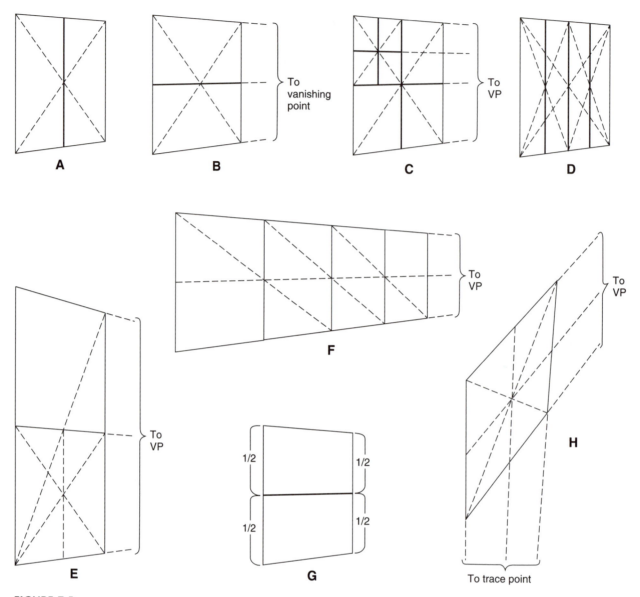

FIGURE 7.5
Finding subdivisions and multiples of the square using the intersection of diagonals.

plane. If two sides of the square are parallel to the picture plane, those sides can be divided into true equal segments in your drawing. The verticals in G are parallel to the picture plane and are divided into two equal-length segments to obtain equal-height top and bottom halves of the square. However, you must draw the diagonals of the square to find the perspective midpoint of the

two horizontal edges, which are not parallel to the picture plane. *Diagonals must be used to find the perspective midpoint of squares that have all edges converging toward vanishing or trace points.* This includes squares in horizontal or inclined planes and squares in vertical planes that are far enough above or below eye level that the vertical sides need to be drawn converging, as in example H.

Squares and Cubes Reference

Translating the square into a cube is the next logical step in establishing three-dimensional proportional relationships. The building in Figure 7.6 uses cubes and parts of cubes as the proportional reference. The portion of the building below the roof line is slightly smaller than one and one-half squares wide on the front and almost two squares on the side (Figure 7.7). Start with the cube in the near corner and extend its sides (A) to establish the approximate proportion of this part of the building. Trim a little on the

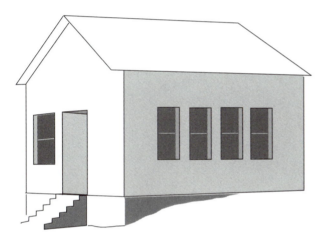

FIGURE 7.6
Cubes or parts of cubes can be used to reconstruct the proportions of this subject.

side to complete the final proportion. The peak of the roof is an additional half-cube height above the main cube. Its apex can be located by extending a vertical through the intersection of diagonals bisecting the building front (B). The size and proportion of other details of the building can be related to those already established (C). For example, the windows on the side are half the height of the main cube. They are centered on the side; the center can be located by the intersection of diagonals drawn from the corners of the side. The door at the front of the building is slightly to the right of the center of the front and about three-fourths of the height of the main corner reference cube.

Of course, it may not be necessary to diagram all these references on your drawing for a subject as simple as the building in our example. Nevertheless, using the square and cube as references greatly facilitates the development of accurate proportions in your drawings.

Using the Square to Determine Ellipse Proportions

Learning to accurately draw a square at any angle to your picture plane is useful in establishing the correct proportion of ellipses for circles. Once the square is drawn in correct perspective rela-

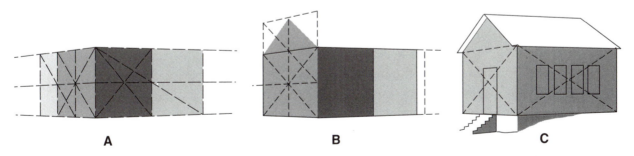

A **B** **C**

FIGURE 7.7
The square and the cube are used to reconstruct the major proportions of the building.

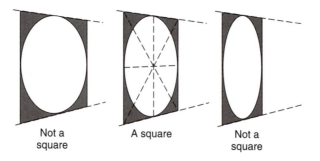

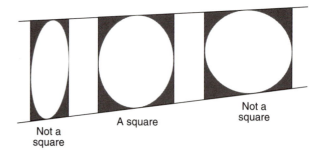

FIGURE 7.8
Using the square to determine the proportion of an ellipse.

FIGURE 7.9
The square (and hence the ellipse) must be correctly related to other perspective elements in the drawing and correctly proportioned.

tive to other elements of the subject, the ellipse always fits within the square. The ellipse is drawn so that its edges touch the perspective midpoints of the sides of the square (Figure 7.8). This ensures that the proportion of the ellipse is correctly related to other parts of the drawing if its enclosing square is correctly proportioned as in the center example in Figure 7.9.

The diagram of the carriage in Figure 7.10 shows the two near wheels within squares that are drawn in the same perspective as other elements in the picture. The convergence and foreshortening are consistent with the perspective of the whole subject. The squares are aligned with the direction in which the wheels are moving. If this were not so, the wheels might appear to be turned, just like the front wheels of a car when rounding a corner. At the very least, the wheels would appear distorted, as in the rendering of the train in Figure 7.11. There the artist has drawn the ellipses in a variety of proportions and has slightly flattened some of them as well. The small ellipses to the far right should be thinner than those to their left. Moreover, the ellipses are not consistent with the direction of the track or with the perspective of the rest of the train.

Establishing the correct proportion of an ellipse when the circle is at various angles to the picture plane is perhaps the most common problem in drawing ellipses that must relate to other

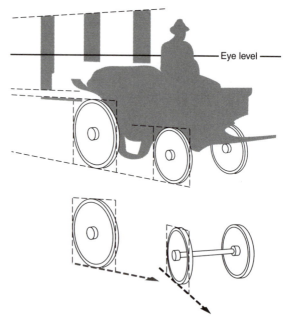

FIGURE 7.10
The proportion of the ellipses is critical if the wheels are to look as if they follow the direction in which the carriage is moving.

(Courtesy, Thunderware, Inc.)

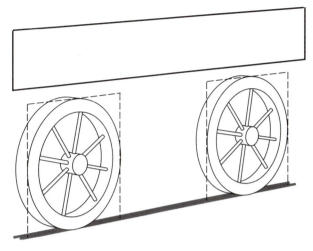

FIGURE 7.12
The convergence of edges and foreshortening in the square must relate to the perspective of the whole before the square can be useful as a guide for drawing an ellipse.

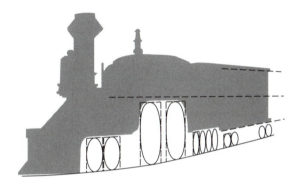

FIGURE 7.11
Ellipses for wheels that are not proportioned consistently with other perspective elements.

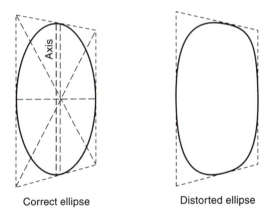

Correct ellipse   Distorted ellipse

FIGURE 7.13
When the square is used to find the ellipse proportion, the ellipse must be drawn without being influenced by the perspective shape of the square.

elements in the drawing. Remember that the plane of the square must be established first and relate to the perspective of the drawing as a whole (Figure 7.12). It is not sufficient to simply adjust the convergence of the square to fit the proportion of the ellipse.

In drawing the ellipse within the square, be careful that the shape of the square does not influence the shape of the ellipse (Figure 7.13). The ellipse touches the square at the square's perspective midpoint on each edge. These tangent points are never at the ends of the major axis and only rarely at the ends of the minor axis. Always make the ellipse symmetrical. Its major axis must be at right angles to the center line of a projected cylinder, as outlined in Chapter 6.

8

Cast Shadows

The shadows cast by objects often help us perceive their form. You can include **cast shadows** in your drawings to give a clearer representation of the objects and to integrate the objects with their surroundings. Cast shadows in subjects are often elusive because of diffusion of the light source, multiple light sources, weak illumination, and reflected light. Even the surface receiving the cast shadow may affect the way the shadow looks. Understanding the basic principles of cast shadow projection will help you to perceive shadows, recognize the variables that can modify them, and use them in your drawings.

The methods for drawing cast shadows vary somewhat, depending on the direction of the light in relationship to the subject and viewer. The schematic in Figure 8.1 identifies the directions we will be discussing.

The terminology used here refers to the direction of the light that illuminates the subject in reference to the artist. Do not be confused by these terms. For example, a **back-lit** subject results from the light source being directly *in front of* the artist, or in back of the subject. A **front-lit** subject results from the light source being directly *behind* the artist, or in front of the subject. Neither back nor front lighting is usually chosen, since both limit the range of values that delineate the form, restricting the form to a flat tone that is either very dark or very light.

A light source located obliquely to the rear of the artist corresponds to what is called **form light** when rendering in light and shade. **Oblique rear light** covers a large segment in Figure 8.1, from near the **side light** direction to almost directly from the rear. A light source located obliquely in front of the artist corresponds to **rim light** in rendering. **Oblique front light** covers a directional quadrant extending from near the side light to almost directly in front of the artist. Just how these various types of lighting affect cast shadow projection is described in this chapter.

Light coming directly from the side is a popular choice in visualizations. This direction provides good form illumination and maximum value range in rendering. What's more, the cast shadows are relatively easy to plot. Most of this chapter is devoted to plotting shadows from side illumination. Side light is a good choice for exploring the principles of cast shadow projection. The same principles apply to other light directions with just a few variations.

Cast Shadows from Side Light

As we describe various projection methods, we will use the term **light ray** to mean a single line from a point representing the light source. In our discussion of side light, the light source is assumed to be the sun. Because the sun is so far away, the light rays from the sun are essentially parallel. For projection purposes, *the rays are treated as parallel to the picture plane and are drawn as parallel lines.*

The cast shadow resulting when light is coming directly from the side, either left or right, is easy to plot if you keep a few things in mind. First, all plotting is based on where the top of a vertical element casts a shadow on a horizontal plane at the base of the vertical (Figure 8.2A). Second, all vertical edges in the subject cast horizontal shadow edges from the base of the vertical. These shadow edges are drawn parallel to the top and bottom of your format. Third, the cast shadow for a vertical ends at the point where the light ray that passes through the top of the vertical intersects the horizontal cast shadow edge from the base of the vertical. A series of verticals would each cast a shadow in the same way, with the light rays projected as parallel lines in the drawing (Figure 8.2B). The edges of the cast shadow are drawn parallel as well.

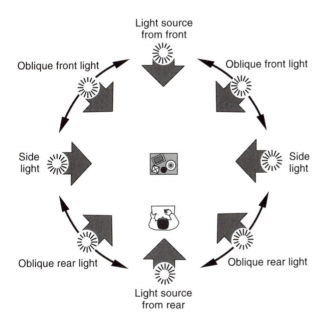

FIGURE 8.1
Direction of light sources relative to the subject and observer.

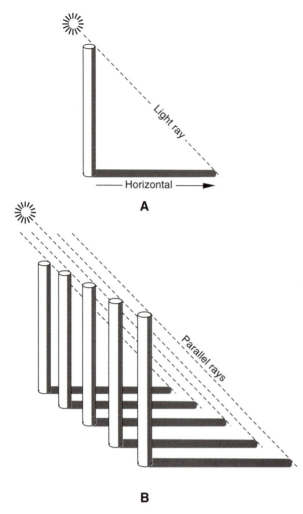

FIGURE 8.2
Side light casts horizontal shadows for the vertical edges in the subject. Light rays are drawn parallel to each other in side light plotting.

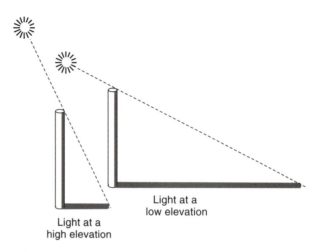

FIGURE 8.3
The elevation of the light source controls the length of the shadow.

The angle of the light ray depends on the elevation of the light source (the sun) from the horizon (eye level). In Figure 8.2, the light source is shown at mid-morning or mid-afternoon. Near noon, with the light source high, the shadows become shorter, and near sunrise or sunset, the shadows become longer (Figure 8.3). Theoretically, at noon, with the sun directly overhead, no shadow would be cast by a vertical edge; at sunset or sunrise a shadow of infinite length would be cast.

To plot the cast shadow for a vertical plane, start with the vertical elements of the plane. A cast shadow for the vertical edge of the plane is drawn as a horizontal from the base of the vertical (Figure 8.4). The point where this horizontal intersects the light ray projected through the top of the vertical determines the length of the shadow cast by that vertical edge. If the top edge of the plane is horizontal, the cast shadow can be drawn toward the same vanishing point as the edge that cast the shadow. *All horizontal edges in the subject cast shadows that project toward the same vanishing points as the edges that cast them.* A shadow edge is projected from the base of the far vertical edge of the plane to intersect the shadow edge cast by the horizontal edge of the plane. A light ray passing through the top of the vertical will also intersect at this point. This completes the outline of the shadow for the vertical plane.

Cast shadows for solids are plotted with the same method (Figure 8.5). Each vertical is plotted as in the previous examples. The cast shadows for verticals in the object appear as horizontals in the drawing. The horizontal edges

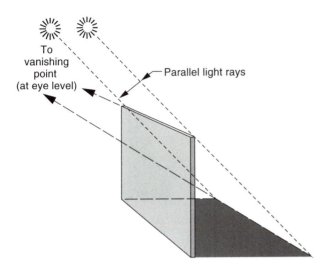

FIGURE 8.4
The shadow cast by a vertical plane is plotted using the two vertical ends of the plane.

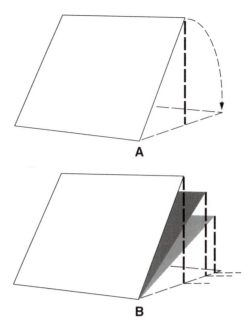

FIGURE 8.6
Find the location on the surface that is the base of a vertical projecting downward from the top of the edge.

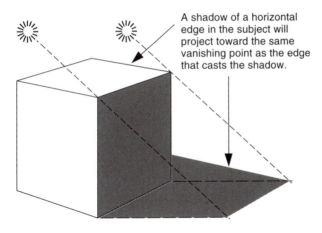

FIGURE 8.5
Shadows for solids are also plotted using the vertical edges to find the length of the shadow.

in the subject, with their cast shadow edges, project toward the same vanishing points at eye level.

Plotting cast shadows would be very simple if all edges in objects were vertical and horizontal and their shadows were cast on horizontal surfaces. When edges are inclined, the vertical dis-

tance from the top of the edge to the surface below must be established. In other words, you must find the exact location in the drawing where you can establish the base of an imaginary vertical projecting downward from the top of the edge (Figure 8.6A). This location is needed to define the direction and length of the cast shadow for the whole edge.

To locate the base of the vertical in the drawing, first establish what direction the inclined edge would take if it were hinged at the base and rotated down to lay flat on the horizontal surface (Figure 8.6A). The direction the edge takes as a horizontal serves as a reference baseline to locate the bottom of the vertical when the plane is in the inclined position. This baseline can serve as an accurate reference at any angle of inclination the plane might be drawn (Figure 8.6B).

A similar method is to consider the inclined edge as one side of a plane that has another side resting on the surface receiving the cast shadow.

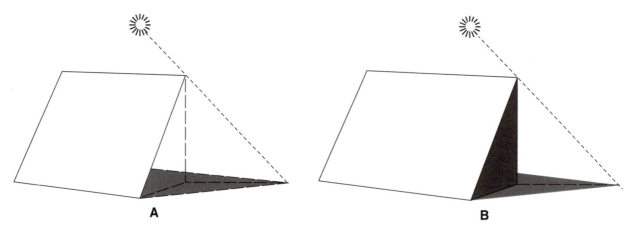

A　　　　　　　　　　　　**B**

FIGURE 8.7
A second method for locating the base of the vertical is to consider the inclined edge as part of a vertical plane that has a horizontal edge resting on the surface receiving the shadow, like the end of the solid shown in B.

In Figure 8.7, the inclined plane shown in A is treated as if it were one side of a wedge-shaped solid with a vertical edge, as shown in B. In the solid, the vertical edge does not cast a shadow, since its projection is enclosed by the shadow of the plane. Nevertheless, the vertical is necessary to plot the endpoint for the shadow of the inclined edge, as in the previous examples. Project the light ray through the top of the vertical to an intersection with a horizontal drawn from the base of the vertical. This locates the shadow for the top of the edge. Since the lower end of the inclined edge is resting on the cast shadow surface, a line drawn from that end to the point plotted for the other end of the edge defines the cast shadow for the inclined edge. The cast shadow for the horizontal top edge of the plane projects from the plotted point toward the same vanishing point as the edge that casts the shadow, since the edge is horizontal.

For shadows cast on nonhorizontal surfaces, the procedure for plotting follows the principles already described. If the shadow is cast on a vertical surface, the plotting is fairly simple. Shadows of verticals in the subject generally parallel the direction of a vertical plane receiving the cast shadow (Figure 8.8).

The cast shadows in Figure 8.8 were plotted exactly as in previous examples, except that the

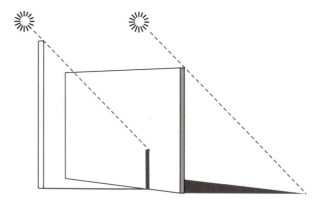

FIGURE 8.8
Shadows from verticals cast on vertical or horizontal surfaces generally follow the direction of the surface.

horizontal cast shadow from the base of the vertical pole, when it reaches the vertical plane, changes to the direction of the plane, in this case vertically. The end of the shadow still intersects the light ray passing through the top of the pole.

The process is slightly more complex when plotting cast shadows falling on inclined planes. If the direction of the surface of the plane is reasonably parallel to your line of vision, you can usually plot the cast shadow as following the slant of the plane, or parallel to the inclined ends of a rectangular plane (Figure 8.9A).

As the cast shadow plane is rotated (Figure 8.9B), with its top and bottom edges no longer near parallel to your line of vision, continuing to

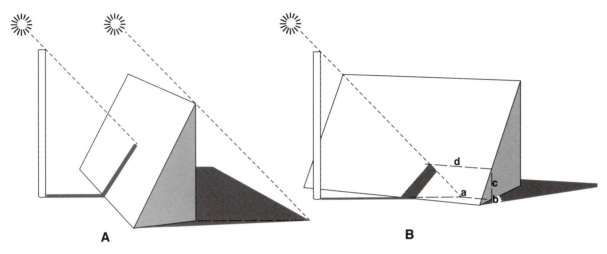

FIGURE 8.9
Shadows of verticals will not follow the angle of an inclined surface except when the plane of the surface is nearly parallel to the line of vision.

follow the slope of the plane would appear to be an obvious error. The shadow on the plane must be plotted. To plot the position of the cast shadow for the top of the vertical pole, project the horizontal from the base of the vertical pole through the inclined plane and continue on the horizontal surface. From the point where the projection intersects the light ray from the top of the pole (point **a** in diagram B), project a line in perspective with the top and bottom edges of the inclined plane to a baseline directly below the inclined edge (point **b**). The baseline is a horizontal edge in perspective, with the same relationship to the inclined plane as in Figures 8.6 and 8.7. From the baseline, project vertically up to the inclined edge (line **c**). Line **c** establishes the vertical height of the inclined plane above point **b**. Line **d** is drawn in perspective at this vertical height, as if it were a line on the inclined plane parallel to its top and bottom edges. The point where line **d** intersects the light ray from the top of the pole is the point on the inclined plane receiving the cast shadow of the end of the vertical. From there, draw the shadow edges to the points where the horizontal part of the shadow intersects the bottom edge of the plane.

The tops and bottoms of verticals can be used as reference points to draw shadows cast by various shapes onto surfaces that are not flat or hori-

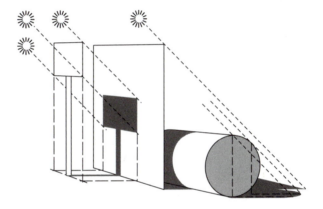

FIGURE 8.10
Shadows cast on irregular surfaces generally follow the contour of the surface.

zontal. The diagram in Figure 8.10 projects the cast shadow of the rectangular sign on a pole onto a vertical plane by extending the vertical edges of the sign to ground level, then horizontally to the bottom edge of the vertical plane that receives part of the cast shadow, then upward to the intersections with light rays passing through the respective top and bottom corners of the sign. This establishes the lateral and vertical position of the cast shadow of the sign and its lateral and vertical dimensions. The shadows for the top and bottom edges move toward the same vanishing point as the horizontal top and bottom edges of the sign.

Verticals drawn from the shadow plane to key points along the edges of other object shapes, as in the end of the cylinder in Figure 8.10, serve as guides for constructing the correct location and shape of their cast shadows. Note that the cast shadow of the vertical edge of the plane, as it falls on the cylinder, closely follows the contour of the cylinder surface.

Around the Box

Constructing cast shadows for even moderately complicated subjects can result in an impressive maze of projection lines, as you can see in Figure 8.11 for the cast shadows of a box. The diagram on the right shows the projections for all the edges of the cast shadow that appear in the final drawing on the left.

Such a construction is not so daunting if taken step by step. Eventually, some steps can be eliminated by short cuts that do not decrease accuracy. However, until you are familiar with the process, it is safer to plot each point on the edge of the subject that causes a change in the direction of the edge of the cast shadow. A good place to begin is at one corner of the subject. Work your way around it progressively, completing the shadow edge as you go. In this example, the sequence begins with the left corner of the drawing and moves counterclockwise around it. Select any angle for the light rays. Remember, they must be parallel to each other throughout the drawing.

In showing the stages involved in plotting the cast shadow, we have cut away parts of the box in Figures 8.12 through 8.14 for clarity. Edge **ab** in Figure 8.12 is not a horizontal edge, so it is necessary to plot the position of the cast shadow for each end of the edge on the horizontal ground plane below in order to find the direction of the cast shadow. The vertical below point **a** is the corner of the box. Projecting a horizontal from the base of the corner until it intersects the light ray through the top of the vertical locates point **a**'s cast shadow at **e** on the ground plane. The other end of the edge point (**b**) is also the top of a vertical extending to the ground plane. Since **ab** is in the same plane as the adjacent end of the box, extending the bottom edge of that plane until it intersects the vertical from **b** locates point **c** on the ground plane. Project a light ray through the top of the vertical **bc**. Where this line intersects a horizontal line drawn from point **c** is where the shadow for point **b** falls on the ground plane at (**d**). A line connecting **d** and **e** is the cast shadow edge on the ground plane for edge **ab**. When **de** intersects the front surface of the box, the shadow changes direction toward point **a** where the edge casting the shadow joins the plane receiving the shadow (Figure 8.13). Line **dfa** is the completed cast shadow edge for **ab**.

Near this corner, the diagram for the shadow on the inside of the box can be plotted, since it

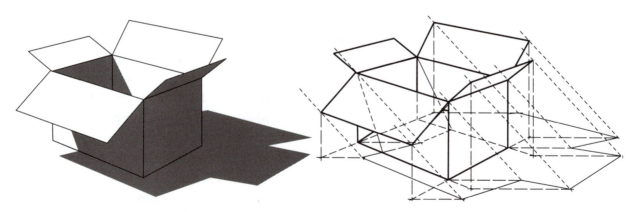

FIGURE 8.11
The shadow cast by a box and the diagram for plotting the shadow outline.

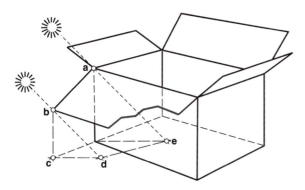

FIGURE 8.12
Both corners of the inclined edge **ab** must be plotted to find the direction of the shadow edge **de**.

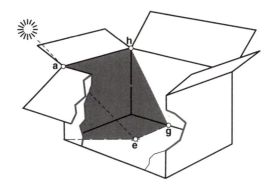

FIGURE 8.14
Plotting the hidden part of the shadow is necessary to find the direction of the visible portion of the cast shadow edge **gh**.

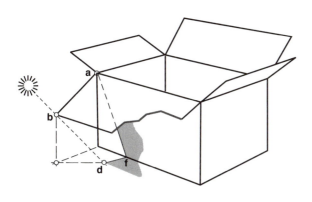

FIGURE 8.13
Part of the edge's shadow is cast on the ground plane and part is cast on the side of the box.

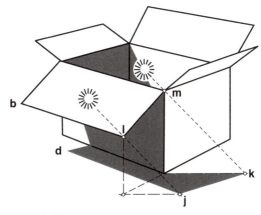

FIGURE 8.15
The corner l must be plotted to find the length of the cast shadow for edge **bl** and the direction of the shadow edge **jk**.

starts with the same plotting point **e** (Figure 8.14). Edge **ah** is a horizontal edge of the box; therefore, its cast shadow projects toward the same vanishing point. Edge **eg** is drawn in that direction until it intersects the back vertical plane of the box; then it turns to point **h,** where the edge that is casting the shadow and the plane receiving it meet. Line **egh** is the cast shadow of edge **ah,** then, and even though the lower portion is hidden by the front vertical plane of the box, all points must be plotted to find the correct location of the part that does show.

Continuing around the outside of the box, shadow edge **dj** (in Figure 8.15) is being cast by a horizontal edge in the box, and it can be drawn through point **d** toward the same vanishing point

as for **bl,** the edge that is casting the shadow. The shadow for point **l** will have to be plotted, however, to find the length of the cast shadow for edge **bl** and to locate the beginning of the cast shadow for the next edge **lm.** Point **k** is located using the vertical of the near corner of the box below **m.** Point **k** is the location of the shadow for point **m.** A line drawn from **j** to **k** is the shadow for edge **lm.**

The shadow edges **de** (Figure 8.12) and **jk** (Figure 8.15), cast by parallel edges in the subject, converge toward a common vanishing point at eye level, since the shadow plane is horizontal. This is not the same vanishing point as for the edges that cast the shadows, however, since those edges in the object are not horizontal.

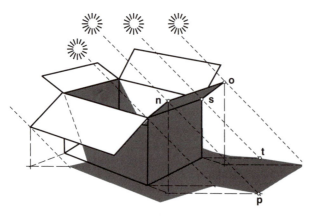

FIGURE 8.16
Plotting key points at the end of the box provides cast shadow directions and lengths for both horizontal and inclined edges.

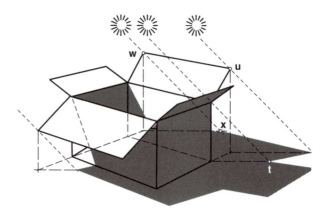

FIGURE 8.17
Plotting the cast shadows of edges at the back of the box completes the visible portion of the shadow area.

The cast shadows for the remaining edges of the box can be plotted in the same manner as previous edges. Edges **pr** (Figure 8.16) and **vx** (Figure 8.17) move toward the same vanishing point as the horizontal edges that cast them. The shadows for the key points on the box, **n, o, u,** and **w,** are plotted to find the cast shadow directions for other edges that are not horizontal in the box.

One Step at a Time

A cast shadow falling on stairs (Figure 8.18) is an interesting problem in shadow projection but not a difficult one to solve if you literally deal with it

one step at a time. In the end, you will find relationships in the shadow projections that cut down the number of individual plottings that need to be done.

This projection problem is typical of stairway drawings that include cast shadows. Shadows cast by the vertical and horizontal elements of the railing fall on two horizontal planes, the first step and top landing. The shadow of the inclined edge of the railing falls on four levels of horizontal planes, starting on the bottom step and ending on the landing, and on three vertical planes, the risers.

The vertical edge of the stair railing is plotted in the usual fashion for verticals (Figure 8.19).

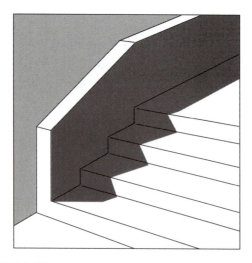

FIGURE 8.18
The stairway and its cast shadow diagram.

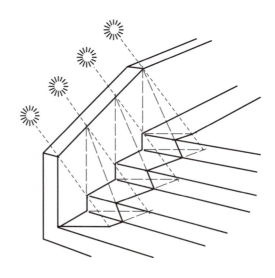

Note that the base of the vertical casting the shadow is at the level of the first step, which is the horizontal shadow plane for the vertical edge. A segment of the cast shadow for the inclined edge of the railing directly above the first step is plotted to find the direction of its cast shadow edge on the horizontal plane of the first step (Figure 8.20). The second vertical **a** starts at the level of the first step. The top of the vertical is its point of intersection with the inclined railing edge; the intersection with the riser behind the first step is ignored up to this point. The direction of the cast

shadow on the riser is treated as if the riser continued upward to the top of the railing and met the other end of the segment of railing casting the shadow (Figure 8.21).

The plotting continues up the stairs (Figure 8.22). It is only necessary to plot from a vertical at the back of each step, since the shadow of one end of the rail segment at each step level was found in the previous plotting. The top landing, in this example, receives the shadow for the point where the inclined and horizontal edges of the railing meet, and a separate plotting for that

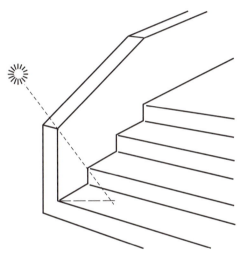

FIGURE 8.19
The vertical edge of the railing casts its shadow at the level of the first step.

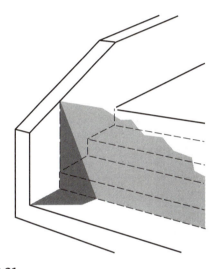

FIGURE 8.21
The edge of the shadow cast on the vertical riser projects toward the top of the vertical used for plotting in Figure 8.20.

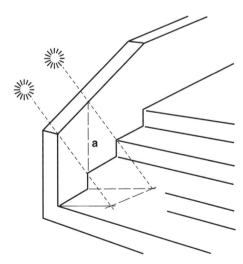

FIGURE 8.20
A vertical is established at the back of the first step to plot the direction of the cast shadow for the inclined edge of the railing.

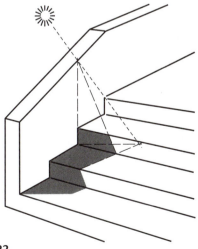

FIGURE 8.22
The plotting is repeated at each step.

point is needed. In this case, a segment of the inclined railing edge casts a shadow on the landing level (Figure 8.23). As before, the cast shadow for the horizontal edge of the railing moves toward the same vanishing point as the edge.

To check the accuracy of your projections, see if the edges of the cast shadow of the railing that fall on the horizontal surfaces of the steps all

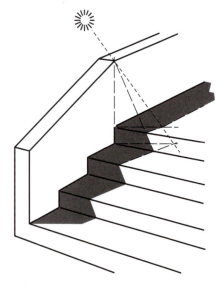

FIGURE 8.23
The cast shadow is plotted separately for the point where the railing changes from an inclined edge to a horizontal edge.

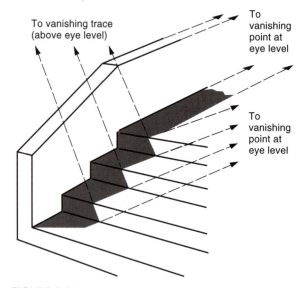

FIGURE 8.24
Shadows cast by a single edge on parallel planes converge toward a common vanishing point. If cast on a horizontal surface, the vanishing point will be at eye level.

project toward a common vanishing point (Figure 8.24). Since the cast shadow is on horizontal planes, the vanishing point is at eye level, but is not the same vanishing point as for other horizontal edges of the subject. The cast shadow edges on the vertical planes of the risers also project toward a common vanishing trace. Remember that for this to hold true, the cast shadow edges must derive from a common straight edge in the subject, and the surfaces receiving the shadow must be parallel planes.

Cast Shadows from Oblique Rear Light

In constructing cast shadows from oblique light, you can follow most of the principles used for side light, with some notable exceptions. With side light projection, lines can be drawn horizontally from the base of the verticals. In oblique light plotting, these projection lines end at a common vanishing point at eye level called a **shadow vanishing point** (Figures 8.25 and 8.26).

For oblique light from the rear, projected light rays through the top of the verticals radiate from a common point directly below the shadow vanishing point. The trace point represents a vanishing point for parallel rays coming from the light source. Lines drawn from the base of verticals to the shadow vanishing point establish the direction of the cast shadow for those verticals. The intersections of these lines with lines drawn from the tops of the verticals to the trace point establish the length of the cast shadows.

The position of the shadow vanishing point to the left or right on the eye-level line depends on the position of the light. If the light comes from directly behind the observer, the shadow vanishing point is directly in front of the observer, or in the middle of the drawing at eye level. As the light source moves to one side of the observer, the shadow vanishing point moves to the opposite side at eye level.

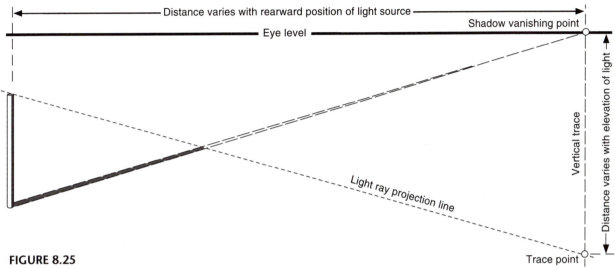

FIGURE 8.25
To find the length of shadows cast by verticals with the light source to the rear, a tract point must be located below the shadow vanishing point.

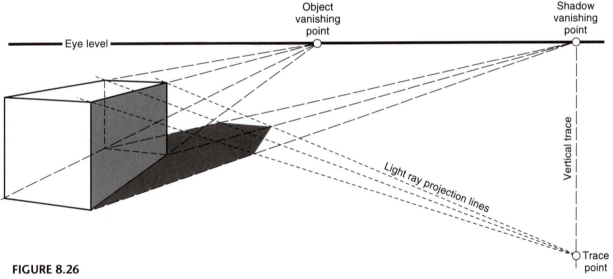

FIGURE 8.26
When the light is from the rear, projection lines radiating from the trace point are used to plot the length of the shadows for vertical elements in solids.

The distance between the trace point and the shadow vanishing point depends on the elevation of the light. The higher the light source, the greater the distance between the trace point and the shadow vanishing point. In early morning or late afternoon, the trace point is close to the shadow vanishing point. The distance between the trace point and the shadow vanishing point increases progressively toward high noon and decreases toward sunset.

Do not confuse object vanishing points with shadow vanishing points. There can be many object vanishing points, one for each set of parallel edges in the subject, but only one shadow vanishing point. The shadow vanishing point is always at eye level when the shadow is cast on a horizontal surface, and the trace point is always directly below it (see Figure 8.26).

As in side light projections, the cast shadow for a horizontal edge in the subject projects toward the same vanishing point as the edge. Cast shadows for parallel inclined edges in the subject project toward a common vanishing point, but not the same vanishing point as the edges. It would be coincidental if any of the edges of the subject or their cast shadows, other than the cast shadows of vertical edges, projected toward the shadow vanishing point.

Cast Shadows from Oblique Front Light

In plotting cast shadows with the light source in front of the observer, the situation is the same as for oblique rear light except that the light source itself is the beginning point for the light rays projecting through the top of verticals, and the shadow vanishing point is located directly below the light source (Figure 8.27). The shadow vanishing point is still at eye level and is the begin-

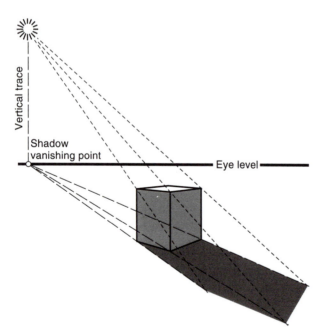

Vertical trace

Shadow vanishing point

Eye level

FIGURE 8.27
When the light source is facing the observer, the shadow vanishing point is at eye level and directly below the light source.

ning point for projections through the bottom of the verticals. As before, the intersection of the two projections through the top and bottom of the vertical edge determines the direction and length of the cast shadow for that edge.

Cast Shadows from Artificial Light

Plotting cast shadows for artificial light requires one major variation from the previous examples: the location of the shadow vanishing point. As in oblique light from the front, the beginning point for the light ray projection through the top of the verticals is the light source itself. The shadow vanishing point is directly below the light source. In artificial light, the shadow vanishing point is not at eye level but at the level of the surface receiving the cast shadow (Figure 8.28).

To locate the exact spot on the surface receiving the shadow vanishing point directly below the light source, you may need to follow the room walls around in perspective with other objects in the drawing, as shown in Figure 8.28. All other methods of plotting the shadow shapes are the same as described for oblique light from the front.

In artificial light, a shadow vanishing point needs to be established at *each* level of *all* planes receiving cast shadows. The shadow vanishing point for the small box in Figure 8.29 is located directly below the light source on the plane receiving the shadow. The shadow vanishing point for the large box is on the plane below this box, on the surface receiving its cast shadow.

Our discussion of cast shadows could not possibly cover all the configurations of objects that cast shadows or all the surfaces that receive them. However, the information given here will enable you to handle most cast shadow projections. Your knowledge of shadow projection will help you understand what you see in the subject and can be a valuable tool in drawing the subject.

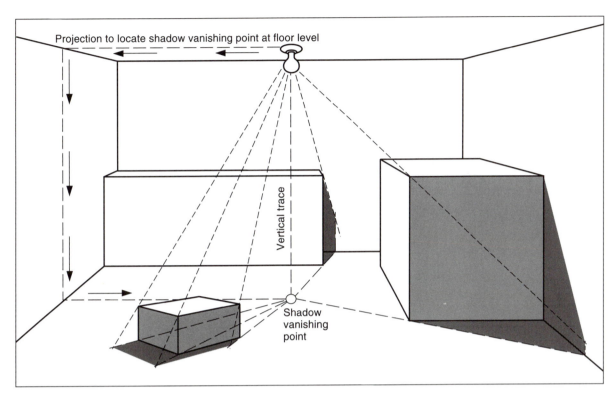

FIGURE 8.28
With artificial light, the shadow vanishing point is located on the surface receiving the cast shadow, directly below the light source.

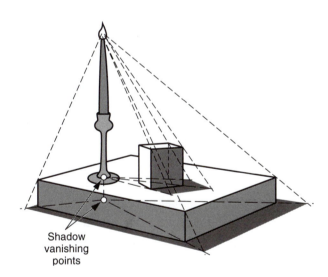

FIGURE 8.29
Shadow vanishing points are established at each surface level that receives a cast shadow.

Mechanical Systems

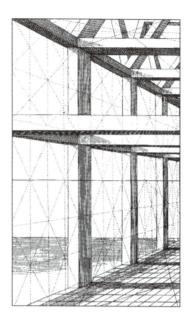

Freehand drawing primarily uses visual assessment to determine the correct foreshortening of planes in the subject when they are viewed at different angles to the picture plane. Use of the square can increase accuracy in freehand drawing. But if very precise proportional relationships are essential, a **mechanical system** may be needed. Usually associated with **technical drawing**, a mechanical system requires appropriate drafting tools, primarily a **T square** and **triangle**, for accurate layout.

The projection layout in Figure A.1 uses a fairly simple mechanical procedure. It provides true foreshortened distances for subjects within a reasonable distance below or above eye level. It does not account for the vertical convergence and foreshortening that occurs if the subject is positioned far below or above eye level.

In the top view of the layout, the distance between the observer (station point) and the subject can vary. Looking down from above in this view, the picture plane is seen as an edge. It is

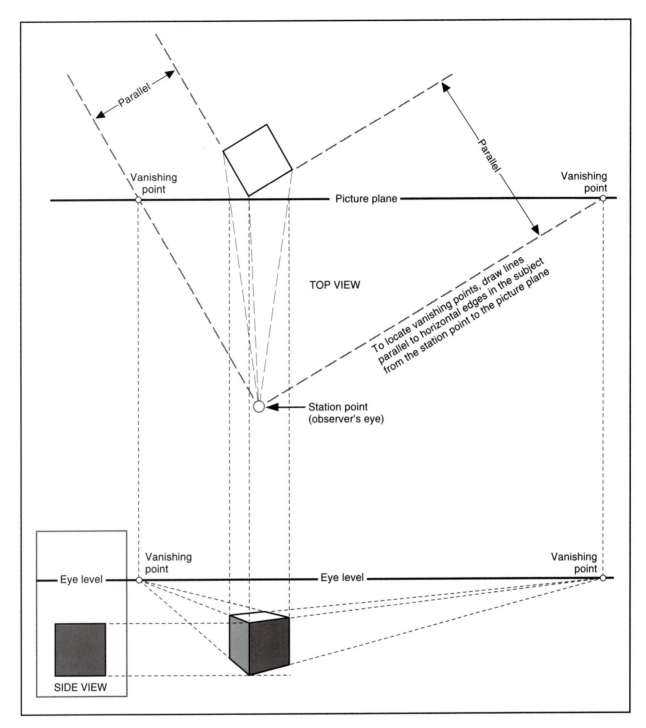

FIGURE A.1
A projection layout for finding foreshortened dimensions and vanishing points for horizontal edges in a subject.

established at right angles to a line of vision between the station point and the subject and must be positioned at the corner of the subject that is nearest to the station point.

To establish the position of the vanishing points for horizontal edges in the main planes of the subject, draw lines from the station point parallel to the edges of those planes. The vanishing points are located where the lines intersect the picture plane.

A side view of the subject also needs to be drawn *in the same scale as the top view* to show the vertical distances of the subject and its position *relative to eye level.* A convenient location for the side view is shown in the illustrated layout. You can then make projections directly from the top and side views to the final drawing.

The eye level from the side view is projected horizontally to become the eye level for the perspective drawing. The vanishing points are projected down from their location on the picture plane. This locates the necessary points to construct the final drawing, as shown in the diagram.

To create the perspective drawing, draw projection lines between the station point and the ends of the edges for each major plane of the subject that is visible to the observer. In Figure A.1, these are the corners of the cube that locate the vertical edges of the two front planes. Where these projection lines intersect on the picture plane establishes the foreshortened dimensions of the planes.

Vertical lines are projected down from the locations on the picture plane of the foreshortened horizontal dimensions of the planes. Lines are

projected horizontally from the side view to obtain the vertical dimension. Note that the side view projection only provides the vertical dimension for the near corner of the subject. From that corner, projections are made to the vanishing points for all other vertical dimensions. The foreshortened distances are established by the projections from the top view.

Correct foreshortening of rectilinear areas in the same plane can be plotted by projection, using points that subdivide a reference rectangle (Figure A.2). The perspective center of the rectangle is first established by the intersection of its diagonals. From the perspective center, draw a line toward the same vanishing point (or points) as the parallel opposite sides of the rectangle, as in view A. Then draw a line from a corner of the plane, passing through the center of the opposite side of the plane to the line projecting toward the vanishing point. This establishes the correct foreshortened width of a second rectangle of the same proportions as the reference rectangle. The projection can be repeated with the second rectangle to find the foreshortening of a third, and continued projections can be made for additional rectangles, as in view B.

Another system can be used to find the relative foreshortening of equal or unequal divisions of a plane, such as a wall of a building divided by panels, doors, or windows (Figure A.3). Draw the near vertical edge of the plane and the eye-level first, and then add projection lines for the top and bottom of the plane toward the vanishing point. Draw a horizontal line through the bottom of the vertical. This horizontal is a baseline to mark the

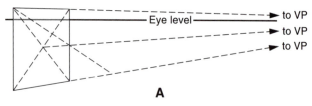

A

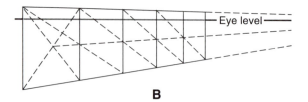

B

FIGURE A.2
Extending multiples of a plane with diagonals.

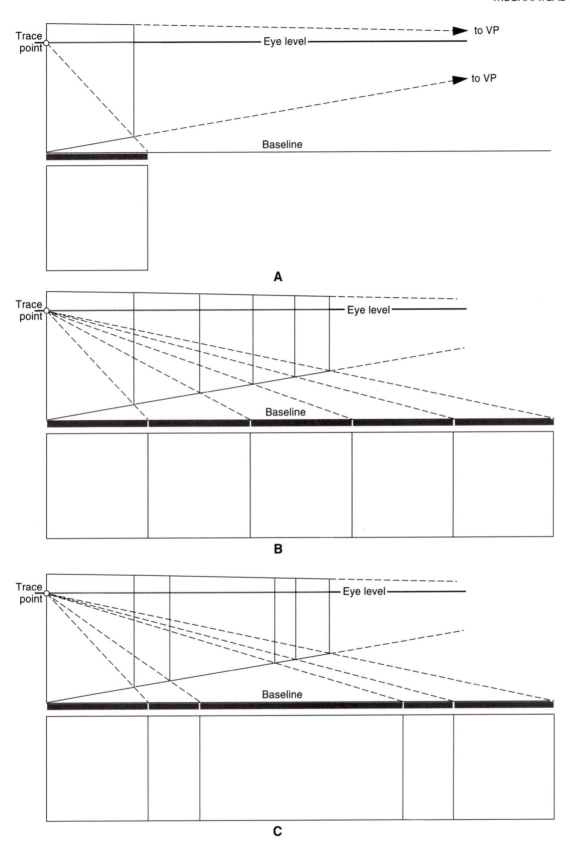

FIGURE A.3
A projection system for finding foreshortened increments in a plane.

true dimensions of the divisions in the plane. The intersection of the vertical and the eye-level line is a trace point for projections of incremental lengths from the baseline, as in view A. Where the projected line from the baseline to the trace point intersects the projection line from the base of the vertical to the vanishing point is the fore-shortened dimension of the plane increment. The increments may be equal in length, as in view B, or unequal in length, as in view C. This projection system provides the relative foreshortened widths of multiple planes or increments within a plane; it does not establish the foreshortened width relative to the height of the plane.

Appendix B

Visualization

Visualization is the process of developing a drawing, an illusion of a three-dimensional object, from information other than the physical object itself. For example, the object you wish to draw might not exist except in your imagination. Or the information you have might be only a two-dimensional plan of the object or a verbal description of it. Or you might want to draw an existing object from a viewpoint that is not available, such as an object in a photograph from a view different than that shown. Artists often use some degree of visualization in their drawings. Many drawings are totally visualized.

In discussing the visualization process, we need to recognize the value of plans as a source of information about the subject. While plans may not prove to be a major resource for you as an artist, plans do convey the precise proportions and locations of the subject elements and are therefore extremely useful in building a perspective drawing.

Plans are usually drawn in a form called **orthographic projection**. You may have seen orthographic projections in periodicals or in plans made by engineers, architects, or other designers. Orthographic projection is a series of two-dimensional views of a subject. Each view depicts one major face of the subject, as if you were looking directly into that face with its planes parallel to the picture plane.

Orthographic views are not drawn with parallel edges converging or distant parts of the subject diminishing in size as is characteristic of perspective drawings. Instead, an orthographic projection—of a cube, for example (Figure B.1)—shows the true proportion of each face of the cube as you would see it if you held the cube and rotated it, looking directly at each of three sides in turn.

To give complete information about a subject, an orthographic projection almost always requires at least two views, often three, and sometimes four or more. For the cube, two views are necessary to know that the object has the same depth, height, and width. A third view is not necessary unless it has detail that does not appear in one of the other views. In Figure B.1, the front of the cube has a square shape on it, the side has a triangle, and the top has a circle. We do not know what the other three sides have on them; if that were important, then additional views would be needed.

Those who make orthographic drawings typically use certain conventions to convey their information. Projection lines may be used to relate edges of the subject in one view with the same edges in another view. **Projection lines** are drawn with long dashes. Edges that cannot be seen in a view because they are behind or within an object are drawn with short dashes and are called **hidden lines.** Cylindrical or conical shapes may have a **center line** in the view showing the side of the cylinder or cone (Figure B.2). One would know that the object was cylindrical in

shape, even with only the side view to work from, because of the center line. Center lines are drawn with alternating short and long dashes.

In this example, we do not need the projection lines and the center line to understand the form of the subject because we have top and side views that provide the information needed. The hidden line is important, however, for otherwise we would not know the depth of the center opening or whether or not it extends the full height of the cylinder.

In Figure B.1, we can understand the major form characteristics of the cube with two views (or one or no view if we know it is a cube). We

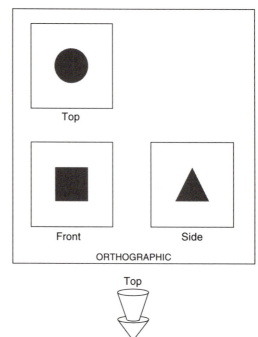

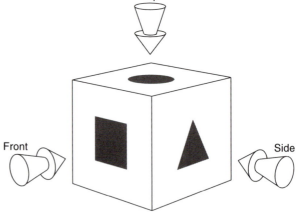

FIGURE B.1
An orthographic projection and a perspective view of the cube.

can understand the cylinder in Figure B.2 from the side view alone, only if the center line is indicated. Based on these views, we can draw these objects in correct proportion and detail from any viewpoint we select. For most objects, however, having only one orthographic view can lead to a variety of interpretations.

In Figure B.3, with only the information shown in the orthographic top view on the left, dozens of interpretations might result. Three that share the same top view are shown. There is no indication of depth in the plan—in fact, the object could also be a flat plane, such as a target.

Having only a side view to work from may also result in a number of interpretations. The two interpretations shown in Figure B.4 share the same side view if seen from the direction of the arrows.

If the two orthographic views shown in Figures B.3 and B.4 were presented as two views of the same subject, there could be only one inter-

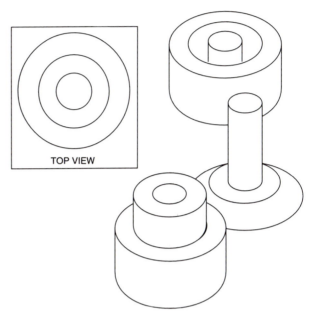

FIGURE B.3
Many interpretations are possible with information from a plan that shows only a top view.

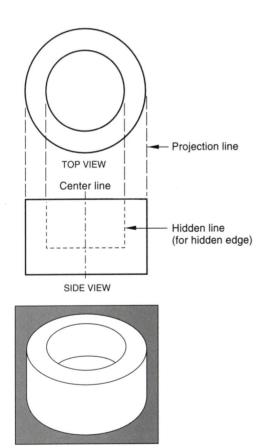

FIGURE B.2
Standard line symbols used in drafting.

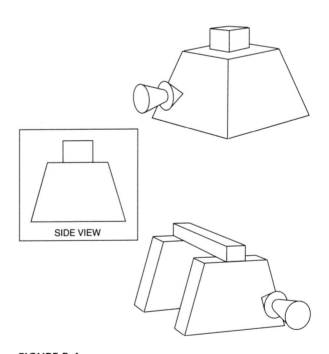

FIGURE B.4
A plan that shows only a side view can also be interpreted in many ways.

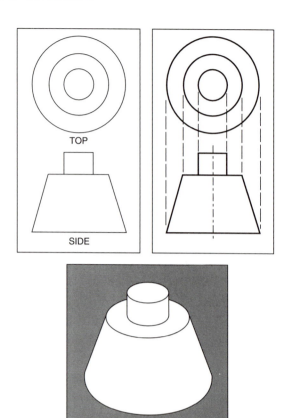

FIGURE B.5
In many cases, two views of a subject will contain all the information necessary to make a perspective drawing.

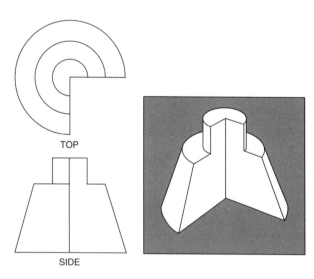

FIGURE B.6
A careful study of all views of a plan is necessary when objects have more complex detail.

pretation of the subject's form (Figure B.5). The top and side views offer adequate information to reconstruct this particular figure. The side view alone with the center line indicated would also be enough.

The side view and center line would not be adequate, however, if the configuration of the object were more complex, as in Figure B.6. Here the top view is available to explain the extent of the section removed from the object. The side view now appears as if we were looking at the object with our line of vision aligned with one of the section planes and at right angles to the other section plane. Together, the top and side orthographic views show all that is necessary to accurately construct the perspective view.

The observer's position in space can be related to the object by establishing the position of the eye level relative to the side view of the plan (Figure B.7). This is often useful to suggest the

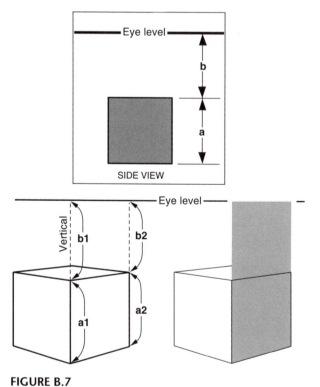

FIGURE B.7
Relating an object to a specific eye level can be accomplished using dimensional increments of the object in the drawing.

size of objects, since the position of the eye level relates the object to human scale. The orthographic plan in Figure B.7 establishes the cube as the same distance below eye level (**b**) as the height of the cube (**a**). In the perspective drawing the near corner of the cube is drawn with the vertical height equal to the distance between the top of the corner and eye level (**a1 = b1**). The other corners of the cube, once the cube is drawn in correct perspective, should also be equal in length to the distance between the top of the corner and eye level (**a2 = b2**). It is as if we have constructed a two-cube-height plane for each side of the cube, with its top at eye level, as in the drawing on the right. Once the correct relationship to eye level is established for one part of the drawing, other parts of the drawing can usually be drawn correctly without constantly having to check their distances from eye level. However, this method is a useful tool for checking the consistency of an object's relationship to eye level when something seems askew.

Some Construction Methods in Visualization Drawing

Practice in visualization drawing is a good test of your understanding of perspective theory and of your skills in interpreting correct proportional relationships among the objects in your drawings. In this section, we provide some helpful hints for laying out the structure of your drawing.

It is often easier to construct more complex objects if you initially simplify the subject to basic geometric forms. In Figure B.8, the basic forms are a rectangular solid and a cylinder. Once the rectangular solid is established (A), detail elements can be carved into it or added on. To accurately locate the cylinder and establish the proportion of its ellipses, first draw an enclosing square for the base of the cylinder on the top surface of the rectangular solid. Then draw the

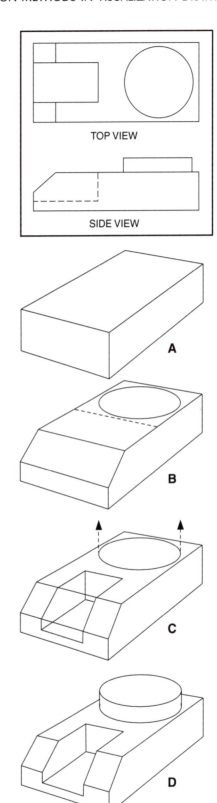

FIGURE B.8
Establishing the structure of the drawing will be much easier if major forms in the subject are first simplified to geometric shapes.

ellipse within the square to obtain the correct ellipse proportion (B). This locates the "footprint" of the cylinder; the rest of the cylinder can be drawn as growing up from the base (C).

In Figure B.9, you need to find the midpoint of a square plane to locate the apex of an equilateral triangle. Draw the square first, using the base of the triangle for one side of the square. Use the

diagonal bisection of the square in perspective to find the true perspective midpoint and the location of the apex of the triangle.

When drawing objects that have a hinge point, such as the pages in a book or the lid of a box (Figure B.10), draw an ellipse that describes the arc of rotation about the hinge; this ensures that any part of the object that follows the arc is accurately foreshortened and in its correct place. The hinge line serves as a center line of a cylinder; the major axis for the ellipse is at a right angle to the hinge line. Other components of the subject may be available to serve as a guide for making the ellipse the right size and proportion. In this example, the cube shape of the box provides two reference points that the ellipse must pass through: the front edge of the box where the lid would be located if closed (**a**) and the base of the box under the hinge (**b**).

Objects often have segments of circular shapes adjoining and tangent to straight edges (Figure B.11). To establish this configuration in perspective, draw the complete ellipse for the cir-

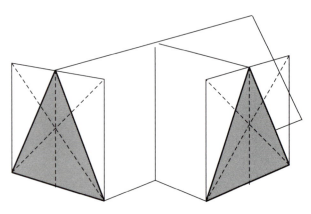

FIGURE B.9
Using the diagonal bisection to find the perspective midpoints of a plane.

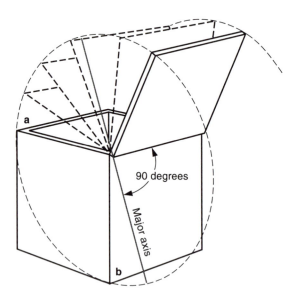

FIGURE B.10
Using an ellipse to find the foreshortened lengths of inclined edges in the subject.

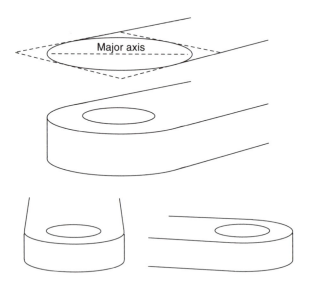

FIGURE B.11
When straight edges are tangent to circles in the subject, different segments of the ellipse are used in the perspective drawing, depending on the viewing angle.

cle first. The straight edge is tangent to the ellipse. Note that different segments of the ellipse are used when the subject is rotated or the viewpoint changes.

Edges that blend with a rounded surface are drawn as if the edge stops inside of the surface boundaries, as in Figure B.12, where the edge fuses with the side of the cylinder. Note that the end of this edge is in line with the tangent point of the ellipse and the straight edges above.

Circular edges that join each other as tangents are more easily constructed if you draw the ellipses for the whole circles first (Figure B.13). Note that different sectors of each ellipse are utilized for the final curve.

When drawing rooms, it is much easier to position and scale objects accurately if the walls and floor are drawn first and a square grid established that is consistent in size throughout (Figure B.14). For example, a grid that is half the distance between the floor and eye level, or one that is keyed to the size of one or more of the principal objects in the room, can function as a reference for relative sizes of objects and their position in the space.

Using the grid on the floor, establish the footprint, or base outline, of each of the objects in the room, such as the chairs, tables, or cabinets, and draw them upward from floor level. The wall grid can be used as a reference for their height.

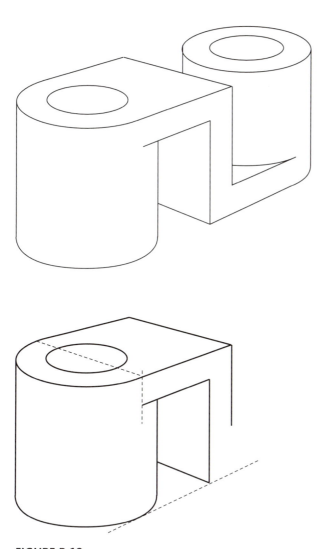

FIGURE B.12
Construction lines may be needed to find the exact stopping point for an edge that blends with the surface of a rounded form.

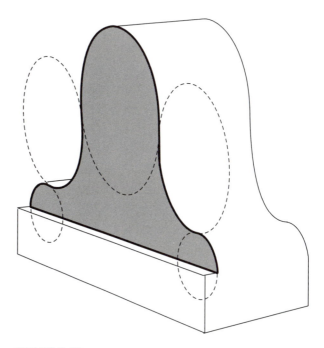

FIGURE B.13
Circular edges that are tangent to other circular edges will use different segments of ellipses when drawn in perspective.

In Figure B.14, note that the angle between the bottom edges of the adjacent walls and a horizontal reference is relatively small, as if you are standing a reasonable distance back from the objects in the room. This is important if you wish to avoid distortion when drawing the furniture nearest to the observer. The eye level has a reference to a known dimension of some object in the room (in this case, twice the height of the table). The table base is a cube in proportion, and one side of the cube is the same size as a square in the floor grid. The shape of the bases of the table and chair is established on the floor using the grid to check the relative sizes and position in perspective. The individual furniture pieces are then drawn from the floor up.

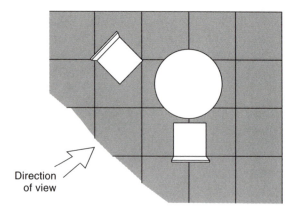

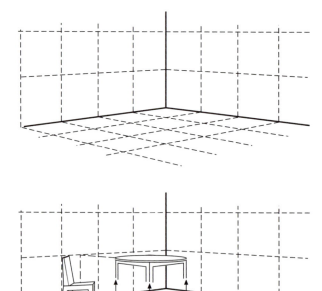

FIGURE B.14

The square grid is used as a reference in positioning and scaling objects in a room. The footprint of the furniture is drawn on the floor first, then drawn upward using the vertical square grid to establish the height.

Glossary

atmospheric perspective A method of creating an illusion of three dimensions with emphasis on the effect of diminishing value contrast, color intensity, and visible detail in a distant subject compared to a nearby subject.

back lit Describing an object when the source of illumination is directly behind it and in front of the observer.

cast shadow The shadow of an object in strong light that falls on the surface below the object or on other nearby objects.

center line In orthographic projection, a dashed line that shows the position of a center line of a circular or cylindrical element in the subject. A center line has a different dash pattern than a hidden line.

concentric circles Circles of different diameter that share the same center point.

convergence The appearance of parallel lines or edges of a subject coming together toward a common point as they move away from the observer.

diagonal A straight line drawn between opposite corners of a rectangle. The intersection of the two diagonals bisecting a rectangle or square is its true center.

ellipse The shape that a circle appears when the plane of the circle is not parallel to the picture plane; a symmetrical oval.

eye level An imaginary horizontal plane exactly at the height of an observer's eyes. The eye level changes as the elevation of the observer's eye changes, but it always remains horizontal.

foreshortening The apparent reduction in the length or width of elements in a subject due to the angle in which they are viewed.

format The drawing area, bounded by drawn borders or the edges of the drawing paper.

form light Light created in rendering when the illumination for the subject is to one side and slightly behind the observer; considered by many artists to create the tonal range and shadows that best delineate the form of the subject.

front lit Describing an object when the source of illumination is directly behind the observer.

hidden lines Dashed lines, used primarily in orthographic projections, that show an edge hidden by another part of the subject.

horizon Another term for *eye level.*

horizontal Describing a level edge or plane, such as the floor of a building or surface of water in a pool, or edges of objects parallel to those edges or planes.

inclined plane A plane that is neither horizontal nor vertical.

landscape orientation A format shape that is wider than it is tall.

light ray In cast shadow plotting, an imaginary straight line between the source of illumination and a key point on the subject. The extension of the ray to the surface below the subject or to a nearby surface will delineate the location of the cast shadow for that point.

linear perspective The method of creating the illusion of a three-dimensional subject, with emphasis on the appearance of edges in the subject as it is viewed in its space and in relationship with other subjects

line of vision An imaginary line between the eye of the artist and the drawing subject. The subject end of the line of vision is usually established near the center of a large subject. One line of vision must be used as a reference throughout the drawing of the subject.

major axis A straight line bisecting an ellipse along its long dimension. The shape of the half-ellipse on one side of the major axis is a mirror image of the half-ellipse on the opposite side.

The major axis is bisected and is at right angles to the minor axis.

mass The physical volume or bulk of a subject. In drawing, it refers to the overall proportion and the space a subject occupies on the drawing page.

mechanical system In perspective drawing, a system using drafting tools to plot grids and projections for a precise layout of perspective elements.

minor axis A straight line bisecting an ellipse along its short dimension. The shape of the half-ellipse on one side of the minor axis is a mirror image of the half-ellipse on the opposite side. The minor axis is bisected and is at right angles to the major axis.

oblique front light A direction of illumination partly between a light to one side and a light directly in front of the observer.

oblique rear light A direction of illumination partly between a light to one side and a light directly behind the observer.

one-point perspective A drawing with one centrally located vanishing point. All parallel, horizontal edges that are at right angles to the observer's picture plane will converge toward that vanishing point. Parallel edges of the subject that are also parallel to the the observer's picture plane will not converge.

orthographic projection A drafting method used by engineers and designers that depicts objects as viewed directly from the top and one or more sides in separate views. Each view shows the object in its true shape without perspective convergence or diminishing sizes.

parallel Being an equal distance apart everywhere. Parallel edges or planes in a subject would never intersect, no matter how far extended. In a drawing of such a subject, parallel edges converge toward a common point, or vanishing point.

perspective center   The true center of a circle or regular rectangle when drawn in perspective. The true center of a square or rectangle is the intersection of diagonals drawn from opposite corners. In a circle, the true center is the intersection of diagonals drawn from the opposite corners of an enclosing square drawn in perspective.

perspective drawing   The method of drawing in two dimensions to create the illusion of a three-dimensional subject.

picture plane   An imaginary transparent reference plane between the observer and subject. The picture plane is always at a right angle to the line of vision.

portrait orientation   A format shape that is taller than it is wide.

projection lines   Layout or reference lines that are not an edge or part of the drawing subject but are used to show how parts are related in different views (as in orthographic projection) or to a reference point (such as a vanishing point in perspective drawing).

proportion   The size of a part compared to the whole or to other parts.

right angle   An angle of 90 degrees between intersecting edges or lines, such as between adjacent sides of a regular rectangle.

rim light   Light created in rendering when the source of illumination is behind the subject or slightly to one side, as with a back-lit subject or one with oblique rear light.

scale   A relative level or degree, usually of size.

set of parallel edges   All the edges in a subject that are parallel to each other. In a drawing of the subject, edges in a set would be drawn receding toward a common vanishing point. Subjects often have several sets of parallel edges.

shadow vanishing point   The common point toward which shadows cast by parallel edges in a subject will converge. Such shadows cast on a horizontal surface will have a shadow vanishing point at eye level.

side light   An illumination source directly to the left or right of the subject and observer.

station point   A fixed location of the observer that remains constant throughout the drawing of a subject.

tangent point   The point of contact between a straight line that lies against, but does not intersect, a curved line.

technical drawing   Precision perspective or isometric drawing used in product design or engineering to show configuration or operation of manufactured objects.

trace line   The same as *vertical trace*.

trace point   The same as *trace vanishing point*.

trace vanishing point   The vanishing point for parallel nonhorizontal edges or lines; a vanishing point not at eye level.

triangle   A drawing tool, usually of plastic, with one angle of 90 degrees and other angles of 45 degrees or 30 and 60 degrees. It is used with a T square to create precise straight-edged shapes or parallel lines.

T square A drawing tool for making straight parallel edges. It is used with triangles to draw other geometric shapes.

vanishing point A reference point in perspective in which the parallel lines in a subject converge.

vertical Describing an upright edge, such as the corners of a building, or an upright plane, such as the side of a building. A vertical is 90 degrees to a horizontal.

vertical trace An imaginary vertical line that intersects a vanishing point on the eye-level line and on which vanishing points for parallel edges in inclined planes will fall.

viewing frame A small mask with an opening the same shape and proportion as the drawing format. The subject is viewed through the opening to relate it to the drawing page.

viewpoint Usually the same as the station point. Viewpoint may also describe a change in viewing direction so that the subject can be seen completely. However, the subject must be drawn as if seen from a fixed location or station point.

visualization Drawing an illusion of a three-dimensional subject as imagined or from information other than a direct view of the subject.

visual perspective A method of creating an illusion of three dimensions with emphasis on the effect of overlapping and diminishing size in a drawing of a subject.

Index